ESTIMATION OF ECONOMIC RELATIONSHIPS FOR INDIAN ECONOMY

ESTIMATION OF ECONOMIC RELATIONSHIPS FOR INDIAN ECONOMY

M. Upender

Foreword by

U. Sankar

KALPAZ

Estimation of Economic Relationships
for Indian Economy

ISBN : 978-81-7835-934-2

Published in 2012 in India by
Kalpaz Publications
C-30, Satyawati Nagar,
Delhi - 110052
E-mail: kalpaz@hotmail.com
Ph.: 9212729499

Laser Type Setting : Rajender Vashist, Delhi
Printed at : G Print Process, Delhi

Contents

Foreword

The major aim of econometrics is to give empirical content to economic relationships. Therefore a good piece of applied econometric research involves statement of an economic problem, specification of an econometric model, establishing links between theoretical constructs and empirically observables, estimation of the model using statistical/econometric methods, testing of hypotheses, reaching inferences, and also giving suggestions for further research.

This book, 'Estimation of Economic Relationships for Indian Economy', by Prof. M Upender, a well-known applied econometrician from Osmania University, contains a collection of papers on six important economic relationships pertaining to Indian economy. The relationships analysed are: (1) output elasticity of employment before and after 1991 economic reform; (2) elasticity of substitution between capital and labour in Indian industries during the pre-reform and post-reform periods; (3) elasticity of employment with respect to real wage rate; (4) tax buoyancy during the pre-reform and post-reform periods; (5) income tax Laffer curve; and (6) existence of long-run equilibrium between India's exports and imports. For investigating each of these relationships, the author motivates the need for giving empirical content in the context of Indian economy and its policy relevance, identifies the relevant theoretical framework and previous literature, specifies hypotheses amenable to statistical testing, estimates the relationships using Indian data and draws inferences based on the empirical results. Readers are introduced to techniques for capturing structural changes in time series and methodologies relating to unit roots, cointegration and error correction mechanism.

Empirical results relating to the employment elasticities and elasticity of substitution between capital before and after the reform are of interest to policy makers and labour economists interested in design of labour policies. The two studies on buoyancy of income tax revenue and determination of India's position in the Laffer curve will be useful to the tax administrators and researchers in public economics in reforming our tax policies. M.Phil., and Ph.D., scholars will benefit not only by learning how fruitful applied econometric research can be done on Indian economic problems but also get inspiration for refining and extending the models and estimating them using recent data and newer techniques.

I commend this concise and lucidly written book to students, researchers, and policy makers in India.

U. Sankar
Honorary Professor,
Madras School of Economics
Chennai-600 025

Ph.D University of Wisconsin, Madison 1967
Asst, Associate, Professor
at University of Wisconsin-Milwaukee
Professor, University of Madras, 1977-95
President, The Indian Econometric Society 1994
Director, Madras School of Economics,1995-99
ICSSR National Fellow, 2003, 2004
UGC Swami Pranavananda Saraswati National
Awardee in Economics-2006

Preface

The present book entitled "Estimation of Economic Relationships for Indian Economy" endows with the sign and size of the empirical values of the economic relationships for the Indian Economy using time series data and cross section data with different techniques. The numerical values of the economic relationships for the Indian Economy help to some extent in understanding the performance of the Economy. The empirical exercises relating to various problematic situations included in the present book were appeared in various national and international journals. I thank the Editors of different journals for having permitted to reproduce my papers in the present volume. I thank Prof U Sankar, Madras School of Economics, India for having written foreword for this book. I thank Prof. S. Satyanarayana, Vice-Chancellor, Osmania University, Prof K.L. Krishna, Delhi School of Economics. Prof. J. Mahender Reddy, Osmania University, Prof. C. Siva Rama Krishna Rao, Kakatiya University and Prof. B. Kamaiah, University of Hyderabad for their encouragement. I also equally thank my colleagues Prof. A.V.S.K.V. Rao, Prof. S. Indrakanth, Prof. B. Shiva Reddy, Prof. T.L.N. Swamy, Prof. G. Ramakrishna, Prof. K. Prathap Reddy, A. Anjaiah (Junior Assistant) and other members of the Department of Economics, Osmania University for their help in the preparation of this petite book. I thank my wife M. Sudha, M.A., (Osmania University) and son M. Sujan, B.E., M.E.(Osmania University) for their help in completing the book. I thank the Dean, Development and UGC Affairs for having sanctioned financial Assistance for publication of this book under XI Plan Merged Schemes for the year 2011-2012. I thank the Management of the Kalpaz Publications, Delhi for publishing the book.

M. Upender

Department of Economics
Osmania University
Hyderabad (AP) India

List of Tables

1

Introduction

It is known fact that the empirical values of the Economic relationships help to some extent in understanding the performance of the economy. The numerical values of the Economic relationships as well help the policy makers either in modifying the existing policies or formulating new policies to do the economy effectively in order to reduce the intensity of problems facing the economies. The present book entitled "Estimation of Economic Relationships for Indian Economy" provides the empirical values of the economic relationships for the Indian Economy using time series data and cross section data.

The empirical values of Economic Relationships on Long Run Equilibrium between Exports and Exports, based on unit root tests, cointegration and Error Correction Mechanism: Output Elasticity of Employment in private and public organised sectors based on demand function for employment generated from the Constant Elasticity of Substitution Production Function; Degree of Tax Buoyancy and differential tax buoyancy with an interaction variable; Effectiveness of the Income Tax Laffer Curve by with and without intercept; Shift in the Elasticity of Substitution in the Indian Industries with an interaction variable under marginal productivity conditions series data having ensured that the Constant Elasticity of Substitution Production Function has a structural shift by Chow-Break point test have been furnished.

The estimation of numerical values of the economic relationships for the Indian Economy is underlying the assumption of *all also equal.*

2

Differential Output Elasticity of Employment During Post Economic Reform Period*

1. Introduction

The concept of output elasticity of employment in a particular sector of the economy helps in understanding the extent of labour absorption capacity of that sector in the Economy. The responsiveness of employment to the changes in output and the presence of structural shift in the responsiveness of employment to the changes in gross output owing to the new economic policy introduced in 1991 in the Indian Economy, needs to be empirically examined. The present study is an attempt in this direction by estimating the empirical demand function for labour, derived from the Constant Elasticity of Substitution production function to comprehend the extent of labour absorption capacity.

2. Data Source

The required annual data on employment in the organised private and public sectors and gross domestic product at factor cost (at 1999-2000 prices) for the period from 1969-70 to 2004-05 is collected from the Handbook of

*Reproduced from the *Singapore Economic Review*, Vol. 56, No. 2, 2011.

Statistics on Indian Economy - 2007 published by the Reserve Bank of India and various issues of Economic Survey brought out by the Ministry of Finance, Economic Division. Government of India. The period after 1991 is considered as post economic reform period to examine the prognostications of economic reforms, initiated by the central government in India, on employment in private and public organised sectors. In view of non availability of the time series data on employment in the unorganised sector, the present study is confined to examine the size and sign of the differential output elasticity of employment in the organised sector by industries only.

3. Empirical Model

The following Constant Elasticity of Substitution [CES] production function is considered in the present paper to derive an empirical demand function for employment.

Specification of the C E S production Function

$$GDP = A\,[\delta\, K^{-\rho} + (1-\delta)\, E^{-\rho}]^{-\eta/\rho} \quad \ldots (1)$$

Where

GDP = Real Gross Domestic Product at factor cost [Output]

K = Capital

E = Employment (Labour)

A = Efficiency parameter ; $A > 0$

η = Returns to Scale parameter; $\eta > 0$

δ = Distribution parameter; $0 < \delta < 1$

η = Extent of substitution parameter, $\rho > -1$,

and related to the elasticity of substitution ;

$\sigma = 1 / 1+ \rho$

marginal product of labour is solved for labour to obtain empirical demand function for labour as follows :

$$\partial GDP/\partial E = \eta\,(1-\delta) / A^{\rho/\eta} \,.\, GDP^{(1+\rho)/\eta} / E^{\rho+1}.$$

$$\eta\,(1-\delta) / A^{\rho/\eta}.\, GDP^{1+\rho/\eta} = E^{\rho+1}$$

$$[\eta\,(1-\delta) / A^{\rho/\eta}.\, GDP^{1+\rho/\eta}]^{1/\rho+1} = E$$

Table 2.2: Sign and Size of Differential Output Elasticity of Employment in Private Organised Sector by Industry [Sample Period: 1979-70 to 2004-05]

Private Sector by Industry	*Intercept [D=0]*	*Differencial Intercept [D=1]*	*Magnitude of employment elasticity [D = 0]*	*Differential employment elasticity [D =1]*	*Magnitude of employment elasticity [D =1]*	R^2	*Adj.*R^2	*F Statistic*	*d*
	β_0	β_2	β_1	β_3	$\beta_1 \pm \beta_3$***				
Agriculture, hunting etc., N = 36	1.0177* [3.586]	0.73904 [1.457]	0.0825* [3.895]	-0.051** [-1.413]	0.0825	0.75	0.732	32.84	1.22
Mining and quarrying N = 36	18.039* [6.514]	-9.3105 [-1.8815]	-1.321* [-6.397]	0.7008** [1.98]	-1.321	0.703	0.673	25.22	0.4
Manufacturing N = 36	1.9588 [0.4798]	-12.070 [-1.6546]	0.135 [0.442]	0.833 [1.597]	Insignificant	0.148	0.068	1.85	2.43
Electricity, gas, Water N = 36	-0.23268 [-0.2506]	-4.997* [-3.013]	-0.0527 [-0.761]	0.3596* [3.034]	0.36	0.40	0.34	7.13	0.79
Construction N = 36	15.006* [7.010]	-9.425* [-2.464]	-1.13* [-7.09]	0.703 [2.57]	-0.427	0.73	0.71	29.43	0.73

Private Sector By Industry	*Intercept [D=0]*	*Differencial Intercept [D=1]*	*Magnitude of employment elasticity [D = 0]*	*Differential employment elasticity [D =1]*	*Magnitude of employment elasticity [D =1]*	R^2	*Adj.R^2*	*F Statistic*	*d*
	β_0	β_2	β_1	β_3	$\beta_1 \pm \beta_3$***				
Whole sale and Retail Trade etc. N = 36	1.880* [4.73]	-4.620* [-2.0776]	-0.06 [-2.08]	0.336* [6.62]	0.276	0.83	0.81	50.52	0.74
Transport, storage and communications N = 36	9.442* [12.29]	-18.72* [-13.633]	-0.74* [-12.85]	1.36* [13.84]	0.62	0.88	0.87	75.94	0.776
Financing, Insurance, real estate## N = 31	-5.817* [-10.158]	-4.308* [-5.08]	0.49* [11.47]	0.31* [5.073]	0.80	0.984	0.983	576.62	1.12

Private Sector By Industry	*Intercept [D=0]*	*Differencial Intercept [D=1]*	*Magnitude of employment elasticity [D = 0]*	*Differential employment elasticity [D =1]*	*Magnitude of employment elasticity [D =1]*	R^2	*Adj.*R^2	*F Statistic*	*d*
	β_0	β_2	β_1	β_3	$\beta_1 \pm \beta_3$***				
Community, Social and Personal services N = 36	-5.811* [-10.158]	-4.308* [-5.08]	0.61 [2.27]	-0.40 [-0.86]	0.61	0.37 6	0.32	6.43	2.08
Private Sector as a whole N = 36	2.246* [8.326]	0.8337 [1.73]	0.15* [7.5]	-0.0569 [-1.65]	0.15	0.93	0.92	133.96	0.42

- d = Durbin-Watson statistic
- Figures within the brackets below the regression coefficients are t values
- * and ** Significant at one and five percent levels respectively
- *** = Since β_2 and β_3 are statistically significant, the sum [$\beta_1 + \beta_3$] or difference [$\beta_1 - \beta_3$] is also deemed to be significant
- ##= Data for this sector is available from 1974-75 only: Sample period 1974-75 to 2004-05
- N = Sample size

5.1: Private Sector

The estimates of differential output elasticity of employment for post reform period and constant employment elasticities for pre reform period in private organised sector are presented in Table 2.2.

The estimate of constant employment elasticity is significantly positive in Agriculture and allied sector during pre reform period revealing that a one percent increase in output is associated with the increase in employment by 0.0825 percent. The regression coefficient of the interaction variable, which is a differential employment elasticity, is insignificant during the post reform period The magnitude of constant employment elasticity during the pre reform period in the mining and quarrying sector is significantly negative and more than unity. The magnitude of differential employment is insignificantly positive. In manufacturing sector, the estimates of the constant employment elasticity during the pre economic reform period and the differential employment elasticity during the post economic reform period are insignificant. In electricity, gas and water industry, the constant employment elasticity is insignificantly negative during the pre reform period. The differential employment elasticity is significantly positive during post reform period showing that a one percent increase in output is associated with the increase in employment by 0.359 percent during the post reform period. In construction industry, the regression coefficients of output during the pre reform period is significantly negative but the coefficient of interaction variable during the post reform period is positively significant showing that the reform measures induced to increase the employment opportunities in construction industry during the post reform period.

In the Trade industry, the constant employment elasticity during the pre reform period is significantly negative. The differential employment elasticity during the post reform period is significantly positive showing that the magnitude of employment elasticity during post economic reform period is 0.276. This leads to the inference that a one percent increase in the output led to increase the employment opportunities by 0.276 percent showing an upward shift in the magnitude of output elasticity of employment in Trade industry during the post economic reform period. In Transport, storage and communications industry the estimate of constant employment elasticity during the pre reform period is, though, significantly negative, the differential employment elasticity during post reform period is significantly positive and more than unity showing an upward shift in employment elasticity during the post reform period in Transport, storage and communications industry. The magnitude of employment elasticity during post reform period is 0.62 illustrating the fact that reform measures induced the employment opportunities in Transport, storage and communications industry. In Financing, insurance and real estate industry the estimates of constant employment elasticity during the pre reform period and differential employment elasticity during the post reform period are positive showing that the magnitude of constant employment elasticity during the post economic reform period is 0.80. This is the only industry that seems to have the moderately high employment elasticity as compared to other industries in the private organised sector evincing that economic growth is relatively more labour intensive in Financing, insurance and real estate industry in India. In Community, social and personal services industry, the magnitude of employment elasticity during the pre reform period is significantly positive during the pre reform period and differential employment elasticity is insignificantly negative during post reform period showing the absence of structural shift. In Organised Private Sector the estimate of employment elasticity during pre reform period is significantly positive while the estimate of differential employment elasticity is insignificantly negative during the post reform period showing the absence of structural shift in organised private sector.

The differential intercepts estimated for the industries of Electricity, Gas, Water, Construction, Whole sale and Retail Trade etc., Transport, storage and communications, Financing, Insurance, the real estate and Community, Social and Personal services in private organised sector are significantly negative showing a downward shift in the average employment during the post economic reform period. The differential intercepts for the industries of Agriculture, hunting etc., Mining and quarrying and Manufacturing are insignificant showing that the average employment remains stable.

5.2: Public Sector

The estimates of differential employment elasticities for the post reform period and constant employment elasticities for pre reform period in public organised sector are presented in Table 2.3.

In Agriculture and Allied sector the employment elasticity during the pre reform period is positively significant showing that a one percent increase in output is associated with the increase in employment opportunities by 0.846 percent. The differential employment elasticity is significantly negative showing a downward shift in employment elasticity during the post economic reform period. The magnitude of employment elasticity during post reform period is – 0.19 showing that a one percent increase in output is associated with the reduction in employment opportunities by 0.19 percent in Agriculture and Allied sector. The employment elasticity during the pre reform period is significantly positive and the differential coefficient of employment elasticity is significantly negative and more than unity in Mining and Quarrying sector during post reform period showing that the reform measures resulted in lessening the employment opportunities by 0.11 percent with the increase in output by one percent.

Table 2.3: Sign and Size of Differential Output Elasticity of Employment in Public Organized Sector by Industry [Sample Period: 1979-70 to 2004-05]

Public Sector by Industry	*Intercept [D=0]*	*Differential Intercept [D=1]*	*Magnitude of employment elasticity [D = 0]*	*Differential employment elasticity [D =1]*	*Magnitude of employment elasticity [D =1]*	R^2	*Adj.* R^2	*F Statistic*	*d*
	β_0	β_2	β_1	β_3	$\beta_1 \pm \beta_3$***				
Agriculture, hunting etc., N = 36	-9.89* [-12.68]	14.341* [10.289]	0.846* [14.53]	1.04* [-10.45]	-0.19	0.90	0.893	98.72	0.82
Mining and quarrying N = 36	-17.57* [-5.575]	21.32* [3.79]	1.45* [6.18]	-1.56* [-3.87]	-0.11	0.61	0.58	16.90	0.27
Manufacturing N = 36	-11.153* [-11.04]	23.18* [12.84]	1.03* [13.63]	-1.68* [13.01]	-0.65	0.88	0.87	78.97	0.29
Electricity, gas, water	-9.82* [-17.123]	13.05* [12.735]	0.87* [20.37]	-0.942* [-12.87]	-0.07	0.96	0.96	276.3	0.48
Construction N = 36	-1.957* [-3.51]	8.866* [8.90]	0.33* [7.73]	-0.64* [-8.97]	-0.31	0.74	0.72	30.79	0.76
Whole sale and Retail Trade etc. N = 36	8.31 [1.64]	-10.54 [-1.16]	-0.59 [-1.57]	0.78 [1.21]	Insignificant	0.094	0.009	1.111	0.71

Public Sector by Industry	Intercept [D=0]	Differential Intercept [D=1]	Magnitude of employment elasticity [D = 0]	Differential employment elasticity [D =1]	Magnitude of employment elasticity [D =1]	R^2	Adj. R^2	F Statistic	d
	β_0	β_2	β_1	β_3	$\beta_1 \pm \beta_3$***				
Transport, storage and communications N = 36	-2.14* [-6.54]	7.16* [12.25]	0.40* [16.55]	-0.52* [-12.37]	-0.12	0.93	0.928	153.4	0.36
Financing, Insurance, real estate## N = 31	-14.94* [-13.95]	15.57* [9.82]	1.26* [15.92]	-1.13* [-9.90]	0.13	0.95	0.949	189.5	0.70
Community, Social and Personal services N = 36	-3.4* [10.43]	7.79* [13.37]	0.57* [23.58]	-0.56* [-13.49]	0.01	0.975	0.973	424.9	0.43
Public Sector as a whole N = 36	-4.03* [-8.14]	10.48* [11.84]	0.67* [18.25]	-0.76* [-11.99]	-0.09	0.95	0.944	196.0	0.34

Notes:

- d = Durbin-Watson statistic
- Figures within the brackets below the regression coefficients are t values
- *and ** Significant at one and five percent levels respectively
- *** = Since β_2 and β_3 are statistically significant, the sum [$\beta_1 + \beta_3$] or difference [$\beta_1 - \beta_3$] is also deemed to be significant
- ## = Data for this sector is available from 1974-75 only: Sample period 1974-75 to 2004-05
- N = Sample size

The estimate of employment elasticity during the pre reform period is significantly positive and close to unity while the differential employment elasticity during the post reform period is significantly negative and more than unity in the Manufacturing sector showing a downward shift. The magnitude of employment elasticity during the pre reform period is significantly positive but the differential employment elasticity during the post reform period is significantly negative in Electricity, Gas and Water industry. In Construction Industry, the estimate of positive employment elasticity during the pre reform period is significant. The estimate of the differential employment elasticity during the post reform period is negatively significant showing that the reform measures resulted in lessening the employment opportunities in Construction Industry by 0.64 percent with the increase in output. The estimates of constant employment elasticity during the pre reform period and the differential employment elasticity during the post reform period are insignificant in Whole sale and Retail Trade Industry. The estimate of employment elasticity during the pre reform period in Transport, storage and communications Industry is positively significant but the estimate of the differential employment elasticity during the post reform period is negatively significant showing that the reform measures resulted in lessening the employment opportunities in Transport, storage and communications Industry by 0.52 percent with the increase in output by one percent. The magnitude of employment elasticity during the pre reform period is significantly positive in Financing, insurance and real estate Industry revealing that a one percent increase in output is associated with the increase in employment by 1.26 percent on the average. The differential employment elasticity is significantly negative and more than unity during the post reform period showing a downward shift in the magnitude of employment elasticity in Financing, insurance and real estate Industry. The magnitude of employment elasticity during the pre reform period is significantly positive. The differential employment elasticity is significantly negative during the post reform period showing that a one percent increase in output is associated with the decrease in employment opportunities by 0.56 in Community, social and personal services Industry in India. In Organised Public Sector, the magnitude of employment elasticity during the pre reform period is significantly positive and differential employment elasticity is significantly negative during the post reform period showing that the magnitude of employment elasticity during the post reform period is -0.09. The reform measures reduced the employment opportunities in public sector during the post reform period as compared to the pre reform period. The differential intercept estimated for the industry of the Whole sale and Retail Trade is insignificant. The differential intercepts are positively significant for other industries showing an upward shift in average employment in the public organised sector.

5.3: Organised Sector (Private and Public Sectors)

The estimates of differential employment elasticities for the post reform period and constant employment elasticities for the pre reform period in organised sector [Private and Public sectors] are presented in Table 2.4.

The employment elasticity during the pre reform period is positively significant in Agriculture and Allied sector and the differential employment elasticity is negatively. The employment elasticity during pre reform period is significantly positive in Mining and Quarrying Industry and the differential coefficient of employment elasticity is significantly negative during the post reform period showing that the reform measures resulted in lessening the employment opportunities in Mining and Quarrying Industry by 0.8 percent with the increase in output by one percent. The estimate of employment elasticity during the pre reform period is significantly positive while the differential employment elasticity during the post reform period is insignificantly negative in the Manufacturing sector. The magnitude of employment elasticity during the pre reform period is significantly positive but the differential

Table 2.4 : Sign and Size of Differential Output Elasticity of Employment in organized Sector [Private and Public] by industry [Sample Period: 1970 to 2005]

Organised Sector by Industry	*Intercept [D=0]*	*Differential Intercept [D=1]*	*Magnitude of employment elasticity [D = 0]*	*Differential employment elasticity [D =1]*	*Magnitude of employment elasticity [D =1]*	R^2	*Adj.*R^2	*F Statistic*	*d*
	β_0	β_2	β_1	β_3	$\beta_1 \pm \beta_3$***				
Agriculture, hunting etc., N = 36	-1.93* [-6.44]	5.32* [9.93]	0.33* [14.89]	-0.38* [-10.04]	-0.05	0.98	0.92	132.65	1.12 2
Mining and quarrying N = 36	-6.64* [-7.04]	11.07* [6.57]	0.66* [9.36]	-0.80* [-6.68]	-0.14	0.79	0.77	39.86	0.44
Manufacturing N = 36	-0.60 [-0.31]	0.81 [0.24]	0.35** [2.42]	-0.076 [-0.31]	0.35	0.20	0.12	2.72	2.18
Electricity, gas, water N = 36	-8.98* [-17.98]	12.01* [13.45]	0.81* [21.83]	-0.87* [-13.58]	-0.06	0.968	0.965	325.3	0.56
Construction N = 36	-0.17 [-0.37]	7.24* [8.51]	0.19* [5.48]	-0.52* [-8.54]	-0.33	0.696	0.668	24.49	0.94
Whole sale and Retail Trade etc N = 36	6.48* [3.31]	-8.41* -2.40]	-0.37* [-2.55]	0.62 [2.47]	0.35		0.17	3.46	0.63
Transport, storage and communications N = 36	-1.72* [-5.72]	6.53* [12.13]	0.37* [16.5]	-0.47* [-12.24]	-0.10	0.937	0.932	161.25	0.38

Organised Sector by Industry	*Intercept [D=0]*	*Differential Intercept [D=1]*	*Magnitude of employment elasticity [D = 0]*	*Differential employment elasticity [D =1]*	*Magnitude of employment elasticity [D =1]*	R^2	*Adj.*R^2	*F Statistic*	*d*
	β_0	β_2	β_1	β_3	$\beta_1 \pm \beta_3$***				
Financing, Insurance, real estate## N = 31	-12.50* [-13.90]	11.34* [8.52]	1.099* [16.5]	-0.821* [-8.59]	0.278	0.965	0.961	248.27	0.69
Community, Social and Personal services N = 36	-3.20* [-9.89]	7.31* [12.65]	0.569* [18.49]	-0.527* [-12.76]	-0.042	0.977	0.975	455.74	0.91
Organized Sector [Private and Public sectors N = 36	1.33* [-3.66]	7.37* [11.33]	0.50* [18.49]	-0.53* [-11.43]	-0.03	0.956	0.952	233.01	0.30

- d = Durbin-Watson statistic
- Figures within the brackets below the regression coefficients are t values
- * and ** Significant at one and five percent levels respectively
- *** = Since β_2 and β_3 are statistically significant, the sum [$\beta_1 + \beta_3$] or difference [$\beta_1 - \beta_3$] is also deemed to be significant
- ## = Data for this sector is available from 1974-75 only: Sample period 1974-75 to 2004-05
- N = Sample size

employment elasticity during the post reform period is significantly negative in Electricity, Gas and Water Industry showing that a one percent increase in output led to decline the employment by 0.87 percent.

In the construction Industry, the estimate of employment elasticity during the pre reform period is positively significant. The estimate of the differential employment elasticity during the post reform period is negatively significant showing that the reform measures resulted in lessening the employment opportunities in Construction Industry by 0.52 percent with the increase in output.

The magnitude of employment elasticity during the pre reform period in Whole sale and Retail Trade Industry is significantly negative while the differential employment elasticity during the post reform period is significantly positive showing that one percent increase in output induced to increase the employment opportunities by 0.62 in Whole sale and Retail Trade Industry.

The estimate of positive employment elasticity during the pre reform period in Transport, storage and communications Industry is significant but the estimate of the differential employment elasticity during the post reform period is negatively significant showing that the reform measures resulted in lessening the employment opportunities in Transport, storage and communications Industry by 0.47 percent with the increase in output.

The employment elasticity during the pre reform period is significantly positive and unity in Financing, insurance and real estate Industry revealing that a one percent increase in output is associated with the increase in employment by 1.1 percent on the average. The differential employment elasticity is significantly negative and less than unity during the post reform period showing a downward shift in the magnitude of employment elasticity in Financing, insurance and real estate Industry.

In Community, social and personal services Industry, the employment elasticity during the pre reform period is significantly positive. The differential employment elasticity is significantly negative during the post reform period showing that a one percent increase in output is associated with the reduction in employment opportunities by 0.527 in Community, social and personal services Industry. The estimate of employment elasticity in organised sector [private and public sectors] is significantly positive during the pre reform period showing that a one percent increase in output led to increase the employment opportunities by 0.50 percent in organised sector. The differential employment elasticity is significantly negative during the post reform period showing that a one percent increase in output is reduced the employment opportunities by 0.53 percent in organised sector. The differential intercepts estimated for the industries of Agriculture, hunting etc., Mining and quarrying, Electricity, gas, water, Construction, Transport, storage and communications, Financing, Insurance, real estate and Community, Social and Personal services are significantly positive showing an upward shift in average employment in organised sector. The differential intercept for the industry of Whole sale and Retail Trade is significantly negative showing a downward shift in the average employment during the post economic reform period and it is insignificant for manufacturing showing that the average employment is stable during the post economic reform period.

6. Conclusion

This paper conducts an empirical test on the differential output elasticity of employment for different industries in the private and public organised sectors of the Indian economy during the post economic reform period by employing a logarithmic form of demand function for employment, derived from the constant elasticity of substitution production function, with the interaction variable, namely, a dummy variable linked to output, having ensured that employment function has a structural shift by chow break test. The empirical results, based on the time series data from the period 1969-70 to 2004-05, show that the positive magnitude of elasticity of employment with respect to output in Transport, storage and communications industry is relatively very high as the differential output elasticity of employment is not only significantly positive but also more than unity followed by Whole sale and Retail Trade and Financing, insurance and real estate industries in the private organised sector during the post economic reform period. This reflects the fact that the labour absorption capacity in the industries of Transport, storage and communications, wholesale and retail, financing, insurance and real estate is relatively high. The magnitude of output elasticity of employment in Financing, insurance and real estate is relatively high during the post economic reform period as the differential output elasticity of employment is relatively small as compared to output elasticity of employment during the pre economic reform period in the private sector. The labour absorption capacity in private sector during post reform period is found to be relatively high as compared to public sector as the differential employment elasticity during the post reform period in private sector is low. Further the results for the organised sector as a whole illustrate that the output elasticity of employment during post reform period is negative on account of negative differential output elasticity of employment showing that the economic growth during the post reform period is not labour intensive in the Indian Economy. Thus the empirical results illustrate the fact that the output elasticities of employment in all sectors are positively very low and negative during the post reform period.Therefore there is a need to review the sector level policies so as to generate more employment opportunities in the organised sector of the Indian Economy.

References

Agarwal R.N., Goldar B.N. (1995), "Economic Reforms and Employment in India-Projections for the Year 2001-02", *Indian Journal of Labour Economics*, Vol. 38, No. 4, pp. 577-95.

Arrow K.J., Chenery H.B., Minhas, B.S. and Solow, R.M., (1961), "Capital - Labour Substitution and Economic Efficiency", *The Review of Economics and Statistics*, Vol. XLIII, No. 3, pp. 225-49.

Papola, T.S. and Alakh N. Sharma (1996), "Structural Adjustment, Poverty, Employment and Safety Nets : The Indian Experience", *Indian Journal of Labour Economics*, Vol. 39, No. 3, pp. 591-623.

Upender M. (1996), "Elasticity of Labour Productivity in Indian Manufacturing", *Economic and Political Weekly*, Vol. 31, No. 21, pp. 7-10.

3

Long Run Equilibrium between Exports and Imports*

1. Introduction

The empirical information on the long run equilibrium relationship between India's exports and imports, the short run disequilibrium and the presence of shift in the magnitude of the error correction in the short run is required to examine the effectiveness of the trade policy of the government of India in reducing the negative trade. There are a large number of empirical studies on exports and imports and their relationship with income and economic growth in India. Some of them are related to income and price elasticities of exports and imports using the macro time series data without testing the stationarity of series [Some of the studies on income and price elasticities of exports and imports include Brar Jaswinder Singh, Da Costa, Kantawala, and Wadhva Charan. As the consistent statistical inference from the estimates of economic relationships based on macro time series depends generally on the assumption of stationarity, it is valid to determine whether time series macro variables are individually stationary or non-stationary. The other studies are related

*Reproduced from the *Applied Econometrics and International Development*, Vol. 7 No. 1, 2007.

to the issue of causality between export growth and economic growth employing the cointegration and error correction procedure. [Some of the studies on causality issue between export growth and economic growth include Geetanjali Nataraj Pravakar Sahoo and Kamaiah, Ramesh Chandra and Malllick]. The present study is vindicated on the grounds that the longer time period (1950-51 to 2007-08) is considered with Augmented Dicky Fuller [ADF] and Phillips-Perron [PP] unit root tests, cointegration [Engel - Granger representation] and error correction model with an interaction variable. The results of the present exercise based on unit root tests, co integration, error correction and shift in the error correction to examine the impact of economic reforms shall be an addition to the existing stock of empirical literature on India's exports and imports. More explicitly, the presence of long run equilibrium relationship between India's exports and imports through the residuals of the cointegration and presence of structural shift in the magnitude of error correction in the short run to capture the impact of economic reforms have been examined.

2. Data Base

Time series annual macro data on Exports (E) and Imports (M) for the period from 1950-51 to 2007-08 in nominal terms have been collected from the Economic Survey [Ministry of Finance, Economic Division] 2008 - 09 and Basic Statistics relating to the Indian Economy - 2008 [Reserve Bank of India] to examine the cointegration between exports and imports.

3. Empirical Methodology

The examination of cointegration between India's exports and imports, requires the determination of the integration order of each time series macro variable. The unit root test, provides the information about the presence / absence of stationarity of the time series variables in levels or first difference If the time series variables, exports and imports, are not stationary in levels, then the series contain unit root. The estimates of economic relationships based on OLS method in the presence of unit root in the levels will be unreliable. The popular methods to detect the presence/ absence of unit root and for determining the order of integration of each variable, exports and imports are the Augmented Dicky Fuller test and Phillips-Perron test. The order of integration of each time series variable needs to be established first. Briefly stated, a time series variable such as E [Exports] and M [Imports] is said to be integrated of order d if it is stationary after differenced d times. This is generally denoted by [E] ~ I(d) and [M] ~ I(d). According to Engel and Granger representation, the two variables E and M, even though they are non stationary in levels, are said to be co integrated, if the residuals from the cointegration regression are integrated of any order less than d. For instance, if [E] ~ I(1) and [M] ~ I (1), the residuals from the co integrating regressions of E on M or M on E have to be I (0) in order to have cointegration between E and M. Then there will be long run equilibrium relationship between E and M. In the short run there may be disequilibrium between actual value of E [or M] and long run equilibrium values. An Error Correction Modeling helps to examine the presence of equilibrium or disequilibrium in the short run. Further, the estimate of error correction term explains the extent of disequilibrium that can be corrected at each period. How quickly disequilibrium can be corrected depends on the magnitude of the estimate of error correction term.

Unit root test in the present exercise is based on the following specifications

ADF Test With trend and intercept:

$\Delta \ln E_t = \text{intercept} + b_1 t + b_2 \ln E_{t-1} + b_3 \Delta \ln E_{t-1} + \text{error}$

$\Delta \ln M_t = \text{intercept} + b_1 t + b_2 \ln M_{t-1} + b_3 \Delta \ln M_{t-1} + \text{error}$

Phillips-Parron Test With trend and intercept:

$\Delta \ln E_t = \text{intercept} + b_1 t + b_2 \ln E_{t-1} + \text{error}$

$\Delta \ln M_t = \text{intercept} + b_1 t + b_2 \ln M_{t-1} + \text{error}$

Where

E = Exports

M = Imports

Δ = first difference operator

Cointegration between Exports and Imports is Based on the following Specification

$\ln E_t$ = intercept + $b_1 \ln M_t$ + error

$b_1 = d \ln E_t / d \ln M_t$ = long run [static] percentage effect

$\ln M_t$ = intercept + $b_1 \ln E_t$ + error

$b_1 = d \ln M_t / d \ln E_t$ = long run [static] percentage effect

ADF and PP tests on residuals [U] are based on the following equations

ΔU_t = intercept + $b_1 t + b_2 U_{t-1} + b_3 \Delta U_{t-1}$ + error

ΔU_t = intercept + $b_1 t + b_2 U_{t-1}$ + error

Where Δ is the fist difference operator

Error Correction and Shift is based on the following Specification

$\Delta \ln E_t$ = intercept + $b_1 \Delta \ln M_t - b_2 EC_{t-1} - b_3 (D^* EC_{t-1})$ + error

- b_2 [Error Correction Term: EC_{t-1}] during pre economic reform period

- b_2 - b_3= (Error Correction Term: EC_{t-1}) during post economic reform period

- b_3=Differential error correction during post economic reform period

$b_1 = \partial \Delta \ln E_t / \partial \Delta \ln M_t$ = Percentage effect in short run

$b_2 = \partial \Delta \ln E_t / \partial EC_{t-1}$ = Proportion of disequilibrium [If it is significantly negative] in t-1 time period can be corrected

$\Delta \ln M_t$= intercept + $b_1 \Delta \ln E_t - b_2 EC_{t-1} - b_3 [D^* EC_{t-1})$+ error

$b_1 = \partial \Delta \ln E_t / \partial \Delta \ln M_t$= Percentage effect in short run

Table 3.1: Stationarity of the Time Series Variables : ADF and PP Test Statistics

Variable	*log level*			*First log difference*		
	ADF Test Statistics	*PP Test Statistics*	*Conclusion*	*ADF Test Statistics*	*PP Test Statistics*	*Conclusion*
1	2	3	4	5	6	7
Exports [E]	-1.88	-1.87	E ~ I (1) Non stationary series	-6.76*	-6.76*	E ~ I (0) stationary series
Imports [M]	-1.44	-1.33	M ~I (1) Non stationary series	-6.92*	-7.07*	M ~I (0) stationary series

Notes:

1. * = Significant at one percent level
2. Mackinnon critical values for rejection of null hypothesis of unit root [non stationarity]

1% Critical Value	-4.13
5% Critical Value	-3.49
10% Critical Value	-3.17

Table 3.2: Stationarity of the Residuals of the Co integrating Regression : ADF and PP Test Statistics

Specification	*Results of Co integration Regression*	*ADF Test Statistic*	*PP Test Statistic*	*Conclusion*		*Annual Growth Rate** (%)*
1	*2*	*3*	*4*	*5*	*6*	*7*
log Exports [E] on log Imports [M]	Ln E= -03978 + 1.011 ln M* [-3.97] [96.6] R^2 =0.994	-3.017*	-3.1005**	$U_t \sim I(0)$	Presence of Co-integration	13.34 Percent
log Imports [M] on log Exports[E]	Ln M =0.4466 + 0.983 ln E* [4.722] [96.6] R^2=0994	-3.0346*	-3.1186**	$U_t \sim I(0)$	Presence of Co-integration	13.18 Percent

Notes:

1. Figures within the brackets below the regression coefficients are t values
2. *= Significant at one percent level
3. *=Negatively Significant at five percent level for rejection of null hypothesis of unit root [non stationarity] in residuals

Critical Value at 1% level	-3.5503
Critical Value at 5% level	-2.9135
Critical Value at 10% level	-2.5945

4. Annual average growth rate is estimated from the ln E or ln M = $b_0 + b_1$ time

$b_2 = \partial \Delta \ln E_t / \partial EC_{t-1}$ = Proportion of disequilibrium [If it is significantly negative] in t-1 time period can be corrected in t-1 period

$-b_2$ [Error Correction Term: EC_{t-1}] during pre economic reform period

$-b_2 - b_3$ = [Error Correction Term: EC_{t-1}] during post economic reform period

$-b_3$ = Differential error correction during post economic reform period

D = Dummy Variable which takes 1 for post economic reform period [After 1992] and 0 for pre economic reform period [Before 1992].

4. Empirical Results

The Augmented Dickey Fuller and Phillips-Perron Unit Root test statistics have been employed to find the stationarity. The results of the same are presented in Table 3.1. The results of the ADF and PP tests show that the time series variables, exports and imports, are non stationary in log levels. Therefore ADF and PP tests have been performed on first log differenced series to find the presence of the stationarity. The results of the ADF test and PP test statistics, show that both the variables are stationary in first differenced form.

As the order of integration of the time series variables, exports and imports, is the identical, the cointegration technique is applied to examine the presence of cointegration of the two variables in the long run. The cointegration regressions of log exports on log imports and log imports on log exports have been run by ordinary least squares method on non stationary time series data. The results of the same are presented in Table 3.2.

With a view to find the degree of integration of the residuals from the cointegratiing regression of exports on imports and imports on exports ADF and PP test statistics have once again been estimated for residuals. Table 3.2 reports the calculated ADF and PP test statistics for the level of the residuals. The calculated ADF and PP test statistics are higher than the MacKinnon critical values showing that the residuals in level form are on a stationary process i.e., they are U ~ I (0). The exports and imports series have unit root in levels while the residuals from co integrated regression have no unit root in levels. Therefore, though the exports and imports series are non stationary in log level form, their linear combination is stationary in level form [Fig. 3.1 and Fig. 3.2] evincing the fact that India's exports and imports are co integrated in the long run. This empirical content (through the Engel - Granger Representation) leads to conclude that there is a long run equilibrium relationship between exports and imports in India during the period under consideration. Further, the regression coefficients on log imports and log exports in two co integrating regressions, constant elasticities, are close to unity with trifling difference, indicating that in the long run one percent of India's imports is synchronised by one percent of India's exports and vice-versa resulting long run trade balance in India. The annual growth rate of the exports is slightly higher than that of imports during the period under consideration.

Even if exports and imports have a tendency to converge towards an equilibrium path in the long run they may diverge from equilibrium path in the short run. The disequilibrium between short run and long run values in lagged year can be corrected by the changes in exports or imports through the trade policies. The effectiveness of trade policies in correcting the disequilibrium has also been examined on the basis of Error Correction Modeling [ECM]. The effective trade policies in correcting the disequilibrium reflects the responsiveness of the changes in exports or imports to previous deviations of actual exports or imports from long run equilibrium. In other words the equilibrium term that entered the ECM as explanatory variable allows to examine the effectiveness of the trade policies to move toward a new equilibrium. With a view to provide an empirical content to this an error correction modeling [ECM] (which combines a long run cointegration relationship and short run corrections of co integrated variables towards the long run equilibrium) has also been attempted to first differenced variables and error correction variable, which are stationary. The results of the same are presented in Table 3.3.

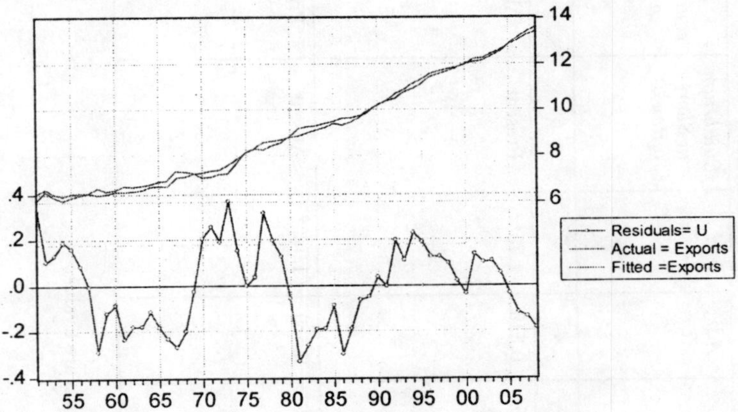

Fig. 3.1: Movements in Risiduals (in E on In M) (1950-51–2007-08)

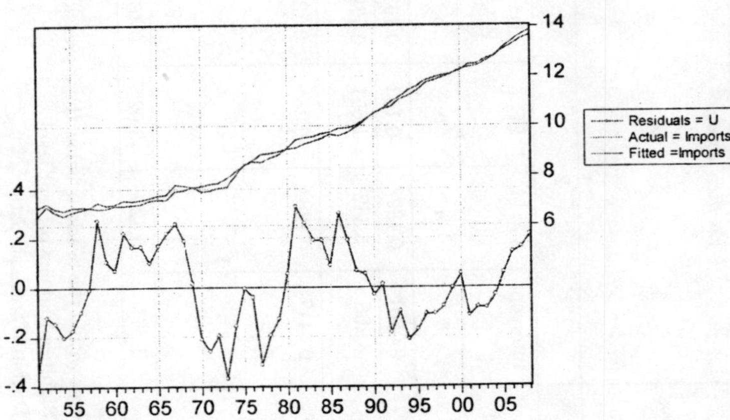

Fig. 3.2. Movements in Risiduals (in M on In E) (1950-51–2007-08)

Table 3.3: Test Statistics for Error Correction Model

Error Correction Specification	*Coefficients on*				R^2	*Adj. R^2*	*d*	*Euilibrium in Short Run*	*Dis-equilibrium in short run*	*Proportion of Error Correction every year*
1	2				3	4	5	6	7	8
ECM - I Δ ln E on Δ ln M, EC_{t-1} and (Dummy* EC_{t-1})	Intercept	Δ ln M_t	EC_{t-1}	D* EC_{t-1}	0.355	0.319	1.75**	Present	Absent	--
	b_0	b_1	b_2	b_3						
	0.0561	0.489*	-0.142	0.161						
	3.208	5.342	-1.651	0.779						
ECM - II Δ ln M on Δ ln E EC_{t-1} and and (Dummy* EC_{t-1})	0.0417	0.728*	-0.28*	0.12	0.422	0.389	1.72**	Absent	Present	28 percent
	1.871	5.429	-3.02*	0.46						

Notes:

1. Figures within the brackets below the regression coefficients are t values
2. * = Significant at one percent level
3. d = Durbin-Watson statistic
4. ** = Absence of Autocorrelation

The regression results based on ECM show that the coefficients on Δ log E and Δ log M, short run elasticities, are significantly positive and less than the coefficients on log E and log M (level variables), long run elasticities, in cointegrating regression evincing the positive effect of additional unit of exports on imports and imports on exports in the short run. The coefficient on Error Correction term (which gives an indication of short run deviations from the long run equilibrium) in ECM is negatively insignificant (ECM - I) evincing the fact that the degree of disequilibrium between short run values and long run values in lagged period is neither corrected nor extended each period showing that there are no disturbances present. Thus, there is equilibrium both in short run and long run periods, evincing the fact that trade policy in India has been effective in maintaining the balance between actual exports and target exports both in the short run and the long run. In the ECM - II, the coefficient on error correction term is negatively significant. This shows that twenty seven percent of disequilibrium in t -1 period is corrected in t period. Thus, though there is disequilibrium between short run and long run about twenty eight percent of the disequilibrium in t-1 period is corrected every year by the changes in imports. The differential coefficient of EC term, b_3, is not significant revealing the fact that the economic reforms could not facilitate to correct more percentage of disequilibrium in the short run. This piece of evidence suggests a need for a review of the trade policy in such a manner that the extent of disequilibrium between short run and long run periods could be eliminated quickly to maintain the equilibrium both in short run and long run in India.

5. Conclusion

The present paper conducts an empirical test on the presence of cointegration between India's exports and imports. The empirical evidence based on cointegration and error correction modeling show that India's exports and imports are co integrated showing the existence of long run equilibrium relationship between them during 1950-51 to 2007- 08 The results based on error correction modeling illustrate that there is a short run equilibrium as well, indicating that the changes in exports adjust to the changes in imports in the same year. There is a disequilibrium between actual values of imports and equilibrium values of imports in the short run. However, twenty eight percent of disequilibrium between long run and short run periods is corrected every year. It should be noted that the differential Error Correction term during post economic reform period is not significant showing absence of shift. On the whole, the presence of cointegration between exports and imports during 1950-51 - 2007-08 implies that India's trade policies have been effective in bringing imports and exports into an equilibrium path in the long run.

References

Brar Jaswinder Singh, "Elasticities of Demand for India's Exports : An Econometric Analysis", *Foreign Trade Review*, Vol. 30, No. 2-3, 1995.

Da Costa G.C., "Elasticities of Demand for Indian Exports - An Empirical Investigation", *The Indian Economic Journal*, Vol. 13, No. 1, 1965.

Engel R.F., and C.W.J. Granger, "Cointegration and Error Correction : Representation, Estimation and Testing", *Econometrica*, Vol. 55, No. 2, March, 1986.

Geetanjali Nataraj, Pravakar Sahoo and B. Kamaiah, "Export-Led Growth in India : What Do the Vars Reveal?", Working Paper-84, Institute for Social and Economic Change, 2001.

Kantawala B.S., "Price and Income Elasticities of Demand for Indian Exports and Imports", *The Indian Economic Journal*, Vol. 43, No. 3, 1996.

Mallick S.K. "Causality Between Exports and Economic Growth In India : Evidence From Cointegration Based on Error Correction Model" *The Indian Journal of Economics*, Vol. LXXVI, No. 302, 1996.

Ramesh Chandra, "Export Growth and Economic Growth: An Investifgation of Causality In India", *The Indian Economic Journal*, Vol. 49, No. 3, Jan-March 2001-2002.

Wadhva Charan D., "Elasticities of Demand for India's Exports and Imports and the Question of the Devaluation of the Indian Rupee", *Foreign Trade Review*, Vol. 8, No. 4, 1974.

4

Differential Elasticity of Substitution in Industries*

1. Introduction

The empirical value of the estimate of differential elasticity of substitution between the capital and labour in the Indian industry is very important to comprehend the extent of substitution possibilities between labour and capital during post economic reform period. There are good number of empirical studies on the elasticity of substitution between labour and capital (Asif Banarji [1975], Goldar [1986], Gujarati [1966], Isher Judge Ahulwalia [1981], Sinha and Sawhney [1970], Upender [1996], Diwan and Gujarati [1968], Mehta [1980], Swamy [1984], Shankar [1970], Umar Kazi [1980], Vijay Basin and Vijay Seth 1977], Sanjib Pohit, Rajesh Chadha, Bina and Sangeeta [1996], and Inderpal Kaur [1997]) in India. The empirical information on differential elasticity of substitution between labour and capital in the Indian Industry during the post economic reform period is required to understand the extent of substitution possibilities during the post economic reform period. Keeping this in view, an attempt has been made to provide empirical content on the estimate of differential elasticity of substitution between labour and capital in the present paper by using the time series data for the period from 1980-81 to 2004-05.

*Reproduced from the *Romanian Journal of Economic Forecasting*, Vol. 6, No. 3, 2009.

2. Empirical Methodology

2.1 : Data Source

The required annual data on production, employment and wages for the period from 1980-81 to 2004-05 has been collected from various issues of Annual Survey of Industries (Factory Sector). The period after 1991 is considered as post economic reform period to examine the prognostications of economic reforms, initiated by the central government in India, on elasticity of substitution between labour and capital in the Indian Industry.

2.2: Variables Used

(i) *Gross Value added [GVA] :* It comprises total ex-factory value of products and by-products manufactured as well as other receipts such as receipts from non-industrial services rendered to others, work done for others on material supplied by them, value of electricity produced and sold, sale value of goods sold in the same condition as purchased, addition in stock of semi- finished goods and own construction] and Net Value Added [NVA] : It is arrived by deducting total input and depreciation from total output] are considered as surrogate for Production [P]

(ii) *Wages to workers [W]:* Wages And Salaries are defined to include all remuneration in monetary terms and also payable more or less regularly in each pay period to workers as compensation for work done during the accounting year. It includes (a) direct wages and salary (i.e., basic wages/salaries, payment of overtime, dearness, compensatory allowance, house rent and other allowances), (b) remuneration for the period not worked (i.e., basic wages, salaries and allowances payable for leave period, paid holiday, lay-off payments and compensation for unemployment, if not paid from sources other than employers), (c) bonuses and ex-gratia payment paid both at regular and less frequent intervals (i.e., incentive bonuses, good attendance bonuses, productive bonuses, profit sharing bonuses, festival or year-end bonuses, etc.). It excludes lay off payments which are made from trust or other special funds set up exclusively for this purpose i.e., payments not made by the employer. It also excludes imputed value of benefits in kind, employer's contribution to old age benefits and other social security charges, direct expenditure on maternity benefits and crèches and other group benefits. Traveling and other expenditure incurred for business purposes and reimbursed by the employer are excluded. The wages are expressed in terms of gross value.

(iii) *Total number of workers (L) :* Workers are defined to include all persons employed directly or through any agency whether for wages or not and engaged in any manufacturing process or in cleaning any part of the machinery or premises used for manufacturing process or in any other kind of work incidental to or connected with the manufacturing process or the subject of the manufacturing process. Labour engaged in the repair & maintenance, or production of fixed assets for factory's own use, or employed for generating electricity, or producing coal, gas etc. are included.] are considered as labour in the present study.

(iv) Labour Productivity (P/L) is measured in terms of gross value added per unit of labour employed and net value added per unit of labour employed.

(v) Wage Rate (W/L) is wage per unit of labour.

2.3: Empirical Model for Differential Elasticity of Substitution

The following constant elasticity of substitution production function has been considered in the present paper to know the extent of substitution possibilities between labour and capital in the Indian Industry. The specification of the constant elasticity of substitution production function is :

$$P = A\,[\delta K^{-\rho} + (1-\delta) L^{-\rho}]^{-1/\rho} \qquad \ldots (1)$$

Where

P = Production [GVA or NVA]

K and L = Capital and Labour inputs respectively.

A = Efficiency parameter

ρ = Extent of substitution between labour and capital related to $\sigma = 1/ 1+ \rho$

δ = Distribution parameter

The above equation has been estimated empirically under the marginal productivity conditions. [Marginal productivity of labour = wage rate]. The marginal productivity of labour is obtained from the above function [equation -1] as follows:

$\partial P/L = A\ [\delta\ K^{-\rho} + (1-\delta)\ L^{-\rho]-1/\rho}\ [\delta\ K^{-\rho}\ (1-\delta)\ L^{-\rho]-1}\ (1-\delta)\ L^{-(1+\rho)}$

$= [P * P^{\rho}] / A^{\rho}\ [1-\delta].\ 1/ L^{1+\rho}$

$= 1\delta/A^{\rho} * P^{1+\rho} * 1/ L^{1+\rho}$

Equilibrium condition between $\partial P/\partial L$ (Marginal Product of labour [MPL] and W/L [Real Wage Rate]) is

$\partial P/\partial L = W / L$

$[1-\delta / A^{\rho}]\ [P / L]^{1+\rho} = W / L$

Solving for [P / L]

$[P/L]^{1+\rho} = [A^{\rho} / (1-\delta)*W/L]$

$[P/L] = [A^{\rho} /(1-\delta)*W/L]^{1/1+\rho}$

Taking logarithms both sides

$\log\ [P/ L] = 1/1+ \rho \log\ [A^{\rho} / 1-\delta] + 1/ 1+ \rho \log\ [W/L]$

$1/1+ \rho \log\ [A^{\rho}/1 - \delta]$ = Constant

$1/1+ \rho = \sigma$ = Elasticity of Substitution or Elasticity of labour productivity with respect to money wage rate.

$\log\ [P / L] = \text{Constant} + \sigma \log\ [W/L]$ . . . (2)

The coefficient on log W/L in the above regression of log P/L on log W/L,ó, is the estimate of constant elasticity of substitution between labour ands capital.

With a view to estimate the magnitude of differential elasticity of substitution between labour and capital during the post economic reform period the model [2] has been extended by taking dummy [D] and interaction variables [D* log $(W / L)_t$] as shown below:

$$\log [P/L]_t = \log \beta_0 + \beta_1 \log [W / L]_t + \beta_2 D + \beta_3 (D * \log [W / L]_t) + \text{error} \quad \ldots (3)$$

Where

$(P/L)_t$ = Labour productivity

$(W/L)_t$ = Money Wage rate

D = Dummy variable that takes value 0 for the years 1980-81 to 1990-91 [Pre economic reform period] and 1 for the years 1991-92 to 2004-05 [Post economic reform period].

β_0 = Intercept during the pre economic reform period (1980-81 to 1990-91), D = 0.

β_2 = Differential intercept during the post economic reform period (1991-92 to 2004-05). D = 1.

β_1 = Magnitude of elasticity of substitution during the pre economic reform period (D = 0)

β_3 = Magnitude of differential elasticity of substitution during the Post economic reform period (D = 1)

As the interaction variable $[D^*\log W/L]_t$ enters the equation in dichotomous form [i.e. = 0 in pre economic reform period and D = 1 in post economic reform period] the derivative of log $[P/L]_t$ with respect to $[D^*\log W/L]_t$ does not exist. Instead, the coefficient of $[D^*\log W/L]_t$ subject to statistical significance, measures the discontinuous effect of the changes in wage rate and economic reforms [policy decisions] [D = 1] represented by the interaction variable on the labour productivity. The variable $[D^*\log W/L]_t$ has been introduced in model to capture the interaction effect of economic reforms and changes in wage rates [cost of labour] on labour productivity The interaction variable takes a value equal to log $[W/L]_t$ during post tax reform period and 0 during pre tax reform period.

The above equation [3] has been estimated by the Ordinary Least Squares method under the equilibrium [marginal product of labour = real wage rate] conditions with one way causation between labour productivity and money wage rate.

2.4: Structural Shift - Chow test

The magnitude of differential elasticity of substitution between labour and capital during the post economic reform period has been examined having ensured that the constant elasticity of substitution production function has a structural shift by chow break point test [F]. The differential coefficient of elasticity of substitution refers to the analysis of, how much the magnitude of elasticity of substitution during the post economic reform period differs from that of pre economic reform period. The results of chow test [F - Statistic] furnished in Table 4.1 show that there is evidence of structural shift in the constant elasticity of substitution production function.

Table 4.1: Search for Structural Shift in CES Production Function

Constant Elasticity of Substitution Production Function *log [P / L] = Constant + σ log [W / L] + error*	*Chow [F] test Statistic*	*No shift in CES Production function during post reform period*
Dependent Variable: log (Gross Value Added / Labour)	12.19	Rejected
Dependent Variable: log (Net Value Added/Labour)	7.52	Rejected

3. Analysis of the Empirical Results

3.1: Degree of variability in labour productivity and wage rates

The coefficient of variation has been estimated to see

the degree of variability in labour productivity and wage rates during pre and post economic reform periods. The summary statistics together with the coefficient of variation are furnished in table 4.2. The degree of variability in labour productivity in case of gross value added is somewhat high as compared to the net value added and wage rates during post tax reform period. The variability is relatively high in labour productivity during post economic reform period as compared to pre economic reform period. The variability in wage rate is very high during pre economic reform period as compared to post economic reform period showing the presence of consistency in wage rate during post economic reform period. The movements in labour productivity and wage rates during pre and post economic reform periods during pre and post tax reform [shaded area] periods are shown in Fig. 4.1.

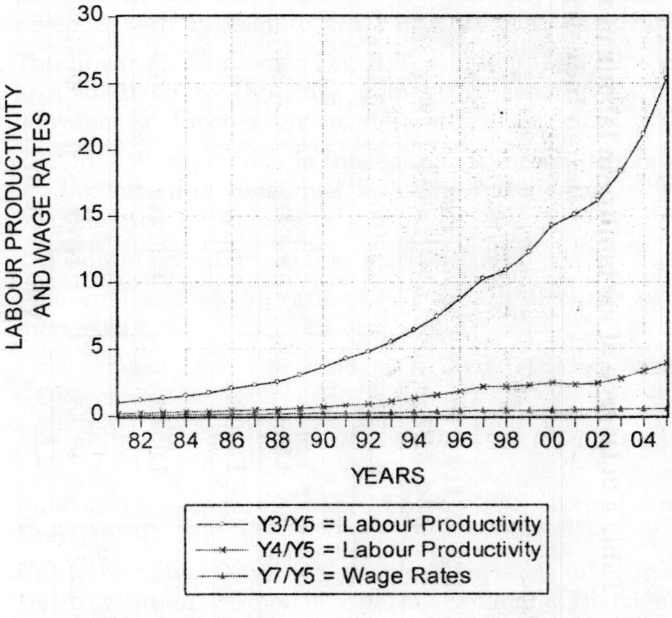

Fig. 4.1: Movements in Labour Productivity and Wage Rates in the Indian Industry 1980-81- 2004-05

Table 4.2: Degree of variability in labour productivity and wage rates in the Indian Industries

Statistic	*Pre economic reform period [1951-1991]*			*Post economic reform period [1992-2005]*		
	Gross Value Added / Labour	*Net Value Added / Labour*	*Wage Rate*	*Gross Value Added / Labour*	*Net Value Added / Labour*	*Wage Rate*
Mean	2.245727	0.430005	0.122459	12.63503	2.186182	0.384841
Median	2.052820	0.387824	0.121875	11.62204	2.234295	0.389634
Maximum	4.289727	0.816753	0.209157	25.34454	3.938402	0.509676
Minimum	1.010222	0.197281	0.015624	4.772594	0.874520	0.216662
Standard Deviation.	1.052203	0.192449	0.055850	6.133743	0.838768	0.094056
Coefficient of Variation (%)	46..85	44.76	45.61	48.55	38.40	24.74

Table 4.3: Differential growth rate of labour productivity [GVA/L and NVA/L] and Wage Rate

Growth rate of the Variable	*Constant β_0*	*Coefficient Time β_1*	*Coefficient Dummy β_2*	*Coefficient of Time* Dummy (3)*	R^2	*Adj.* R^2	*d*
Log (GVA/L)	0.012483	0.139737*	0.288113*	-0.018553*	0.998227	0.997973	1.077390
t-values	0.496282	32.86782	4.904322	-3.582896			
Log (NVA//L])	-1.594905*	0.132465*	0.629736*	-0.036928*		0.987726	0.933287
t-values	-27.42520	13.47563	4.636238	-3.084328	0.989260		
log (W / L)	-3.172221*	0.182262*	1.106818*	-0.120597*		0.892625	1.260241
t-values	-20.99711	7.137187	3.136641	-3.877224	0.906047		

Notes: Estimates are based on the following equations:

log [GVA/L} = $\beta_0 + \beta_1$ time + β_2 D + β_3 (D * time) + error

log [NVA/L] = $\beta_0 + \beta_1$ time + β_2 D + β_3 (D * time) + error

log [W/L] = $\beta_0 + \beta_1$ time + β_2 D + β_3 (D * time) + error

Annual average growth rate during the pre economic reform period=β_1

3.2: Growth rates of the labour productivity and wage rates

The growth rates of labour productivity and wage rates during the pre economic reform period and differential growth rates of labour productivity and wage rates during the post economic reform period have been worked out having ensured that there is a structural shift in the growth rates by chow break point test statistics (F - Statistic in case of [1] GVA/L = 12.19: [2] NVA/L = 11.29 and [3] W/L = 7.52). The growth rates are set out in table 4.3.

The growth rate of the labour productivity [ratio of gross value added to labour employed] is 13.97% per annum during pre economic reform period. The differential growth rate is significantly negative showing a down ward shift in the growth rate during the post economic reform period. The growth rate of the labour productivity [ratio of net value added to labour employed] is 13.24% per annum during pre economic reform period. The differential growth rate is significantly negative showing a down ward shift in the growth rate of the labour productivity during the post economic reform period The growth rate of the wage rate is 18.22 % per annum during pre economic reform period. The differential growth rate is significantly negative showing a down ward shift in the growth rate of wage rate during the post economic reform period.

3.3: Estimates of Differential Elasticity of Substitution

The regression results of the Constant Elasticity of Substitution Production Function fitted to the time series for the Indian Economy have been set out in table 4.4.

The regression results of the constant elasticity of substitution production function with the ratio of gross value added to labour [GVA/L] as the dependent variable illustrate that the coefficient of money wage rate [labour cost], known as the elasticity of labour productivity with respect to wage

Table 4.4 : CES Production Function: Differential Elasticity of Substitution

Dependent Variable	*Constant*	*Coefficient of Dummy*	*Coefficient log (W/L)*	*Coefficient Dummy* log (W/L)*	*Elasticity of substitution during post economic reform period*	*R^2*	*Adj. R^2*	*Durbin-Watson statistic*
	$log\ \beta_0$	β_2	β_1	β_3	$\beta_1 \pm \beta_{13}$**			
Log (GVA/L)	1.955873*	2.289851*	0.550532*	1.299290*	1.87	0.966781	0.962036	0.880574
t-values	9.682914	7.990231	6.434936	5.988609				
Log (NVA/L)	0.265517	1.939732*	0.529919*	0.989485*	1.52	0.969314	0.964930	1.177111
t-values	1.455724	7.495740	6.859485	5.050675				

Notes:

- * Significant at one percent level.
- ** = Since β_1 and β_3 are statistically significant, the sum $[\beta_1 + \beta_3]$ or difference $[\beta_1 - \beta_3]$ is also deemed to be statistically significant

rate, is positive but less than unity during pre economic reform period in the Indian Economy illuminating that labour productivity is relatively inelastic to the changes in money wage rates. This shows that a one percent increase in money wage rate is leads to increase the labour productivity by 0.55 percent. The differential elasticity of substitution is significantly positive and more than unity more than unity during the post economic reform period. The constant elasticity of substitution during the post economic reform period is also more than unity evincing the fact that the substitution possibilities are more in favour of labour in the Indian industries [factory sector] during post economic reform period. The estimate of the elasticity of substitution during the post economic reform period implies that a one percent increase in wage rate will lead to increase the labour productivity by 1.8 percent in the Indian Industries.

The regression results of the constant elasticity of substitution production function with the ratio of net value added to labour [NVA/L] as the dependent variable furnished in table 4.3 illustrate that the coefficient of money wage rate, the elasticity of labour productivity with respect to wage rate, is also significantly positive and less than unity during pre economic reform period in the Indian Industry. The differential elasticity of substitution is more or less unity. The sum of elasticity of substitution during the pre economic reform period and differential elasticity of substitution during the post economic reform period is 1.5 showing that a one percent increase in money wage rate leads to increase the labour productivity more than one percent. This leads to deduce the fact that the substitution possibilities are more in favour of labour in the Indian industries [factory sector].

4. Conclusion

This paper conducts an empirical test on the differential elasticitiy of substitution between labour and capital in the Indian Industry during the post economic reform period by employing a logarithmic form of constant elasticity of substitution production function with two different dependent variables, namely, the ratio of gross value added to labour and net value added to labour, having ensured that constant elasticity of substitution production function has a structural shift by chow break test. The differential elasticity of substitution is significantly positive and more than unity during the post economic reform period when the ratio of gross value added to labour is considered as dependent variable and close to unity when the ratio of net value added to labour is considered as dependent variable. The sum of the elasticity of substitution during pre economic reform period and differential elasticity of substitution during post economic reform period exceeds unity evincing the fact that substitution possibilities are relatively more in favour of labour in the Indian industry during the post economic reform period.

References

Arrow, H.B. Chenery B.S. Minhas and R.M. Solow, "Capital-Labour Substitution and Economic Efficiency," *The Review of Economics and Statistics*, August 1961.

Asif Banarji, *Capital Intensity and Productivity in Indian Industry*, MacMillan Co., New Delhi, 1975.

Cobb, C.W. and Douglas P.H., "Theory of production", *American Economic Review*, Vol. XVIII, 1928.

Diwan R.K. and D.N. Gujarati, "Employment and Productivity in Indian Industries – Some Questions of the Theory and Policy", *Artha Vijnana*, Vol. 10, No. 1, March, 1968, pp. 29-67.

Goldar, B.N. *Productivity Growth in Indian Industry*, Allied, New Delhi, 1986.

Gregory C. Chow, "Tests of Equality between sets of Coefficients in two linear Regressions", *Econometrica*, Vol. 28, No. 3, 1960.

Gujarati, D.N. "A Test of ACMS Production Function: Indian Industries" 1958, *Indian Journal of Industrial Relations*, Vol. 2, No. 1, 1966, pp. 95-97.

Inderpal Kaur, *Impact of Liberalisation on Indian Industry*, Deep & Deep Publications, New Delhi, 1997.

Isher Judge Ahulwalia, *Productivity Growth in Indian Manufacturing*, Oxford University Press, 1981.

Krishna K.L. (Ed.) *Econometric Applications in India*, Oxford University Press, 1997.

Mehta, S.S. Productivity, *Production Function and Technical Change – A Survey of Some Indian Industries*, Concept Publishing Co., New Delhi, 1980.

Panchamukhi, V.R., "A Survey of Econometric Studies in the fields of Production, International Trade and Money and Banking" in A Survey of Research in Economics, Vol. VII, *Econometrics* [ICSSR] Allied, 1978.

Sanjib Pohit, Rajesh Chadha, P.L. Bina and N. Sangeeta, Estimation of Substitution Parameter in Indian Industries, *National Council of Applied Economic Research*, New Delhi, 1996.

Shankar, U. Elasticities of Substitution and Returns to Scale in Indian Manufacturing Industries, *International Economic Review*, Vol. II, No. 3, October 1970, pp. 399-411.

Sinha, J.N. and P.K. Sawhney, *Wages and Productivity in Selected Indian Industries*, Vikas Publications, 1970.

Swamy, T.L.N. "Factor Substitution in Indian Industries: Some Cross-Section Evidence", *Margin*, January 1984, pp. 31-38.

Umar, A. Kazi, The VES Production Function: A Case Study for Indian Manufacturing Industries, Oxford Economic Papers, Vol. 32, No. 1, March, 1980, pp. 163-75.

Upender, M. Elasticity of Labour Productivity in Indian Manufacturing Sector", *Economic and Political Weekly,* Vol. XXXI, No. 21, May 25, 1996, pp. M-7-M10.

Vijay, K. Basin and Vijay K. Seth, "Estimation of Production Functions for Indian Manufacturing Sector", *Artha Vignana*, Vol. 19, No. 2, June 1977, pp. 113-28.

5

Degree of Tax Buoyancy*

1. Objective of the Exercise and Data Source

Its well known fact that increase in the tax revenue in the Indian Tax System is due to increase in the national income and the tax policy decisions of the government. The total response of the tax system due to the above two factors that is increase in the national income and the tax policy decisions of the government is known as the tax buoyancy. With a view to provide an empirical content to the tax buoyancy during post tax reform period in the Indian Tax System, an attempt has been made in the present exercise using the data available up to date. More specifically the present paper looks at the sign and size of the differential coefficient of tax [revenue] buoyancy during post tax reform period in India by fitting a double-log regression model with an interaction variable to the stationary time series data based on Augmented - Dicky Fuller [ADF] and Phillips-Parron [PP] Tests. The period after 1992 is considered as post tax reform period to look at the prognostications of tax reforms that had been initiated by the government of India. The annual actual data points on gross central tax revenue [GTR_t] and gross domestic product [GDP_t] at current market prices [Income] from 1950-51 to 2004-05 [Fifty Five Financial Years] have been taken from the Indian Public

*Reproduced from the *International Journal of Applied Econometrics and Quantitative Studies*, Vol. 5, No. 2, 2008.

Finance Statistics 2005-2006 [Ministry of Finance, Department of Economic Affairs, Economic Division], Handbook of Statistics on Indian Economy 2005-06 [Reserve Bank of India] and Economic Survey 2006- 2007 [Ministry of Finance, Economic Division]. The differential constant tax buoyancy refers to as how much the constant tax buoyancy coefficient of post tax reform period's tax revenue function differs from the constant tax buoyancy coefficient of pre tax reform period's tax revenue function. Though there are number of empirical studies on the degree of tax buoyancy in India based on time series data [Some of the influential studies include Amaresh Bagchi [1994], Dwivedi, D.N., [1996] Govinda Rao, M., [2000] Purohit, M.C., [1978] Rao, V.G., [1979] Sahota, G.S., [1961] Sury, 1978] M.Upender, M., [2002] *Infra, References*], the present study will be an addition to the existing literature on tax buoyancy in the Indian Tax System as the degree of tax buoyancy during pre tax reform period and degree of differential tax buoyancy during post tax reform period have been examined having ensured that the variables log (GTR_t) and log (GDP_t) are stationary time series by Augmented-Dicky fuller and Phillips-Parron tests.

2. Augmented - Dicky Fuller and Phillips-Parron Tests

As the consistent statistical deductions from macro time series data depend by and large on the assumption of stationarity, it is perceptive to determine whether time series variables, log (GTR_t) and log (GDP_t), are individually stationary or non-stationary. If they are non-stationary, then the concern is to what degree/order they are non-stationary. Therefore the order of integration of each time series variable is examined by the Augmented - Dicky Fuller [ADF] and Phillips-Parron [PP] Tests in levels on log (GTR_t) and log (GDP_t) before estimating the coefficients of tax buoyancy during pre tax reform period and differential tax buoyancy during post tax reform period by ordinary least squares method. If the calculated ADF and PP statistics are more than the critical values then the variables [log (GTR_t)

Table 5.1: ADF and PP Unit Root Test Statistics (1950-1951 to 2004-05)

Variable	*log level*		
	ADF Test	*PP Test*	*Conclusion*
1	*2*	*3*	*4*
GDP	-3.843011*	-3.720697*	GDP ~ I (0) Stationary series
GTR	-3.463132**	-3.463132**	GTR ~ I (0) Stationary series

Notes:

1. *and ** Negatively Significant at five and ten percent levels respectively
2. Mackinnon critical values for rejection of null hypothesis of unit root [non stationarity]

Critical Value at 1% level	-4.1348
Critical Value at 5% level	-3.4935
Critical Value at 10% level	-3.1753

and log (GDP_t)] are said to be stationary or integrated to the order zero in log levels i.e., log $(GTR_t) \sim I(0)$ and $\log(GDP_t) \sim I(0)$. If the calculated ADF and PP statistics are less than the critical values then the time series variables [$\log(GTR_t)$ and $\log(GDP_t)$] are said to be non-stationary in log levels. Then ADF and PP tests shall be performed on the first difference of log (GTR_t) and log (GDP_t) [i.e., ADF and PP unit root tests on "log (GTR_t) = log GTR_t – log GTR_{t-1} and "log (GDP_t)= log GDP_t – log GDP_{t-1}]. If log GTR and log GDP are found to be stationary in first difference then they are integrated to the order one i.e., log (GTR) ~ I (1) and log (GDP) ~ I (1). Indeed the ADF and PP unit root tests in first difference have not been performed in the present exercise as the ADF and PP statistics in levels are found to be significantly negative. The results of the ADF and PP tests with constant and trend are presented in table 5.1.

The ADF and PP unit root tests [in level] on log GTR and log GDP are based on the following specifications with trend and intercept.

ADF test

$$\Delta [\log (GTR_t)] = \text{constant} + \beta_1 \log (GTR_t (-1)) + \beta_2 \Delta [\log (GTR_t (-1))] + \beta_3 \text{ Trend} + \text{error} \quad \ldots \text{(I)}$$

$$\Delta [\log (GDP_t)] = \text{constant} + \beta_1 \log (GDPt(-1)] + \beta_2 \Delta (\log(GDP_t(-1))] + \beta_3 \text{ Trend} + \text{error} \ldots \text{(II)}$$

PP test

$$\Delta [\log (GTR_t)] = \text{constant} + \beta_1 \log (GTR_t (-1)) + \beta_2 \text{ Trend} + \text{error} \quad \ldots \text{(III)}$$

$$\Delta [\log (GDP_t)] = \text{constant} + \beta_1 \log (GDP_t(-1)) + \beta_2 \text{ Trend} + \text{error} \quad \ldots \text{(IV)}$$

Where

GDP_t= gross domestic product [GDP_t] at current market prices [Income]

GTR_t= gross central tax revenue [GTR_t] I

Δ = first difference [operator] of the log of the variable [log (GTR_t) or log (GDP_t)].

The null hypothesis that the time series variable [log (GTR_t) and log (GDP_t)] has a unit root [i.e., it is non stationary] is rejected as b_1, [the regression coefficient of log (GTR_t(-1)) in equations I and III and the regression coefficient of log (GDP_t(-1)), in equations II and IV] is significantly negative. The results illustrate that the non stationarity / unit root could be rejected for the log levels of the variable as the calculated ADF and PP statistics are more than the critical values. Therefore the time series variables [log (GTR) and log (GDP)] in log levels are stationary ie., log (GTR_t) ~ I(0) and log (GDP_t) ~ I (0).

3: Empirical Model for degree of Tax Buoyancy and Differential Tax Buoyancy

The degree of differential gross tax buoyancy during post tax reform period has been examined by fitting the following specification [Equation – V] with an interaction variable [D*logGDP_t] to the stationary time series data.

$$\log GTR_t = \log \beta_0 + \beta_1 \log GDP_t + \beta_2 D + \beta_3 (D * \log GDP_t) + \text{error} \quad \ldots (V)$$

Where

GTR_t = Gross Tax Revenue in nominal terms [Rs. crore]

GDP_t = Gross Domestic Product at market prices (Typically in the empirical studies the GDP [Income] is taken as base) [Rs crore]

D = Dummy Variable [D = 0 for pre tax reform period and D = 1 for post tax reform period]

D*GDP= interaction variable to capture the combined effect of the changes in income and tax policy decisions

β_0 = Intercept during pre tax reform period [D = 0]

β_2 = Differential intercept during post tax reform period [D = 1]

If the regression coefficient of dummy variable [D], β_2, is significantly positive then the average gross tax revenues go up; If it is significantly negative, then the average gross tax revenues go down during post tax reform period [D =1]

β_1 = Magnitude of tax buoyancy during pre tax reform period (D = 0) : $\beta_1 > 0$.

β_3 = Magnitude of differential tax buoyancy during post tax reform period (D = 1); β_3 more than or less than zero subject to the statistical significance evincing the presence or absence of difference between the magnitude of tax buoyancy during post tax reform period and magnitude of tax buoyancy during pre tax reform period.

$(\beta_1 \pm \beta_3)$ = Magnitude of tax buoyancy during post tax reform period (D = 1).

β_1 = regression coefficient of tax buoyancy [(1 > 0] during pre-tax reform period when D = 0.

β_3 = differential coefficient of tax buoyancy [(3 more than or less than 0] that allows a shift [an upward / a downward] in the gross tax buoyancy during post tax reform period when D =1.

As the interaction variable [D*log GDPt] enters the equation in dichotomous form [i.e., D = 0 in pre tax reform period and D = 1 in post tax reform period] the derivative of log GTRt with respect to [D*log GDPt] does not exist. Instead, the coefficient of [D*log GDPt] subject to statistical significance, measures the discontinuous effect of the changes in income and tax policy decisions [D = 1] represented by the interaction variable on the gross tax revenue. The variable [D*log GDP_t has been introduced in model [equation – V] to capture the interaction effect of tax reforms and changes in income on gross tax revenue from major taxes. The interaction variable takes a value equal to log GDPt during post tax reform period and 0 during pre tax reform period. If b1* ± b3* more than or less than b1* then there will be an upward or a downward shift in the degree of gross tax buoyancy during post tax reform period. If $\beta_1{}^* + \beta_3{}^{**}$ = (1*, then the magnitude of tax buoyancy remains the same in pre and post tax reform periods implying the absence of shift. Where * and ** denote statistically significant and insignificant respectively.

4. Analysis of the Empirical Results

4.1: Degree of variability in gross tax revenue and income

The coefficient of variation has been estimated to see the degree of variability in Gross Tax Revenue and Income during pre and post tax reform periods. The summary statistics together with the coefficient of variation are furnished in table 5.2. The degree of variability in gross income is somewhat high as compared to the gross tax revenue during post tax reform period. The variability is relatively high in gross tax revenue as compared to gross income during pre tax reform period. The variability in gross income and gross tax revenue is very high during pre tax reform period as compared to post tax reform period showing the presence of consistency in gross income and

Table 5.2: Degree of Variability in Gross Tax Revenue and Income

Statistic	*Pre tax reform period [1951-1991]*		*Post tax reform period [1992-2005]*	
	GTR	*GDP*	*GTR*	*GDP*
Mean	10687.83	111808.9	154116.1	1698512
Median	3206.000	45677.00	141508.5	1631766
Maximum	57577.00	568674.0	304958.0	3126596
Minimum	405.0000	9934.000	67361.00	653117.0
Standard Deviation	14937.59	141195.1	71194.10	779297.2
Coefficient of Variation (%)	45.88	46.195	139.76	126.28

gross tax revenue during post tax reform period. The movements in Tax revenue and Income during pre and post tax reform [shaded area] periods are shown in Fig. 5.1.

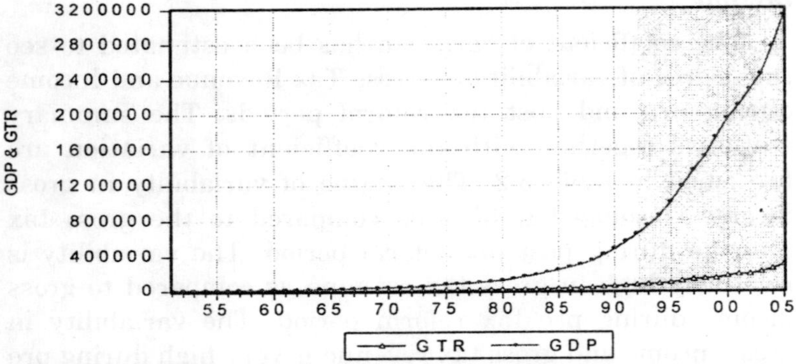

Fig. 5.1. Movements in Tax Revenue and Income

4.2: Search for Structural shift in Gross Tax Revenue Function

With a view to search for structural shift in the gross tax revenue function between pre and post tax reform periods,the chow break point test [Gregory C Chow, 1960] has been applied. The estimate of F ratio, 52.7145, [Chow test] based on the regression equation log [GTR] = log β_0+ β_1 log [GDP] is more than the table value evincing the fact that there is a shift in the tax revenue function between pre and post reform Periods. The dummy variable and interaction variables have been used in the tax revenue function [equation-V] to scan presence/absence of differential intercept and differential tax buoyancy during post tax reform period as the chow test does not affirm whether the shift is due to intercept or coefficient of the gross income.

4.3: Degree of Tax Buoyancy

The degree of tax buoyancy during pre tax reform period and differential tax buoyancy during post tax reform period have been estimated by fitting a double log regression model [Equation –V] by OLS method as the time series log

Table 5.3 : Degree of Tax Buoyancy during pre and post tax reform periods in India

Intercept [D = 0]	*Differential intercept [D =1]*	*Size of tax buoyancy [D = 0]*	*Differential tax buoyancy [D =1]*	*Size of tax buoyancy [D =1]*	R^2	*Adj.*R^2	*Durbin-Watson Statistic*
β_0*	β_2*	β_1*	β_3*	$\beta_1 \pm \beta_3$**			
-5.23 [-35.28]	3.67 [4.25]	1.23 [91.50]	-0.29 [-4.84]	0.94	0.9975	0.9973	0.7051

Notes:

- Figures within the brackets beneath the regression coefficients are t values
- * Significant at one percent level.
- ** = Since β_1 and β_3 are statistically significant, the sum $[\beta_1 + \beta_3]$ or difference $[\beta_1 - \beta_3]$ is also deemed to be statistically significant
- Coefficient of log GDP_t, β_1, is the estimate of tax buoyancy during pre tax reform period i.e., when D = 0

  $\log GTR_t = \log \beta_0 + \beta_1 \log GDP_t$

  where $\beta_1 = d \log GTR_t / d \log GDP_t$ is the tax buoyancy during pre tax reform period
- when D =1 [post tax reform period] $\log GTR_t = [\beta_0 + \beta_2] + [\beta_1 \pm \beta_3] \log GDP_t$,

  where $[\beta_1 \pm \beta_3] = d \log GTR_t / \log GDP_t$, is the magnitude of tax buoyancy during post tax reform period

variables are found stationary in the log levels, log (GTR_t) ~ I(0) and log (GDP_t) ~ I (0). The results are presented in table 5.3.

The regression results illustrate that the estimate of constant gross tax buoyancy is positively significant and more than unity during pre tax reform period illuminating that gross tax is relatively elastic. From this result it can be comprehend that, on the average, a one percent increase in income accompanies with more than one percent increase in gross tax revenue all else equal. Further it can be understood that the average propensity to tax [ratio of GTR to GDP] was increasing with the increase in GDP during pre tax reform period. The regression coefficient of interaction variable is significantly negative and stumpy showing a downward shift in the degree of tax buoyancy during post tax reform period. The estimate of the tax buoyancy, which was just above the unity, during pre tax reform period is less than unity during post tax reform period evincing the fact that the gross Tax is relatively inelastic. From this it can also be understood that the average propensity to tax [ratio of GTR to GDP] is declining with the increase in GDP during post tax reform period. With a view to provide empirical content to this the following specification is also fitted to the data, The results of the same are furnished below:

$$[GTR/GDP] = \text{constant} + \beta_1 D + \beta_2 GDP + \beta_3 [D*GDP] + \text{error.}$$

β_2 = Rate of change in average propensity to tax per a unit change in income [GDP] during pre tax reform period

β_3 = Differential Rate of change in average propensity to tax per a unit change in income [GDP] during post tax reform period

$$[GTR/GDP]_t = 0.061395^* + 0.034484\ D^* + 1.20E\text{-}07GDPt^* -1.22E\text{-}07\ (D * GDP_t)^*$$

$$t = [23.93483]\ [3.896687]\ [8.338709]\ [-8.115233]$$

$R^2 = 0.63$

$R^2 = 0.61$

Durbin-Watson Statistic = 0.38

Note = * Significant at one percent level

The visual plot [Fig. 5.2] based on time series data also confirms the same.

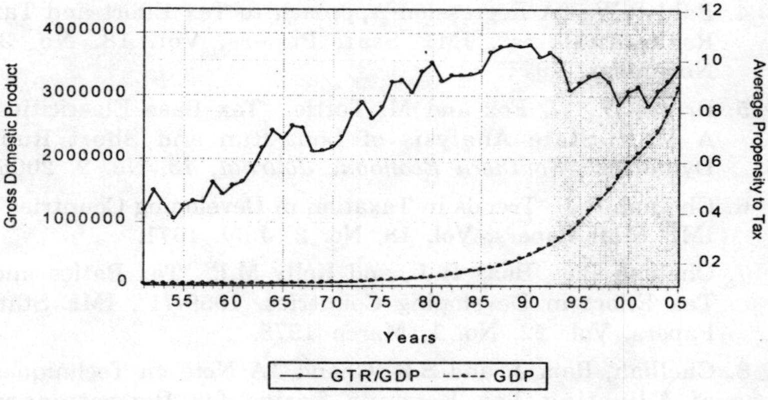

Fig. 5.2: Movements in the Average Propensity to Tax with increase in Income (1950-51 to 2004-05

5. Conclusion

The empirical results of the present exercise, based on the stationary time series macro annual data for the period from 1950-51 to 2004-05, elucidate that the gross tax buoyancy estimate is just above the unity during pre tax reform period evincing the fact that the ratio of Gross Tax Revenue to Gross Domestic Product was increasing with the increase in Gross Domestic Product during pre tax reform period and is less than unity during post tax reform evincing the fact that the ratio of Gross Tax Revenue to Gross Domestic Product is declining with the increase in Gross Domestic Product during post tax reform period.

References

1. Amaresh Bagchi, "India's Tax Reforms: A Progress Report", *Economic and Political Weekly*, Vol. XXIX, No. 43, October 22, 1994.
2. Andreoni, J., Erard, B., and Feinstein, J., "Tax Compliance", *Journal of Economic Literature*, June, Vol. 36, 1998.
3. Ansari M., "Determinants of Tax Ratio: A Cross-Country Analysis", *Economic and Political Weekly*, June 19, 1982.
4. Bahl R.W., "A Regression Approach to Tax Effort and Tax Ratio Analysis", IMF Staff Papers, Vol. 18, No. 3, November, 1971.
5. Bruce, D., W. Fox and M. Tuttle, "Tax Base Elasticities: A Multi-State Analysis of Long-Run and Short Run-Dynamics", *Southern Economic Journal*, 73, No. 2, 2006.
6. Chelliah R.J. "Trends in Taxation in Developing Countries", IMF Staff Papers, Vol. 18, No. 2, July, 1971.
7. Chelliah R.J., Baas H.J., and Kelly M.R. "Tax Ratios and Tax Effort in Developing Countries, 1969-71", IMF Staff Papers, Vol. 22, No. 1, March 1975.
8. Chelliah, Raja J. and S.K. Chand, "A Note on Techniques of Adjusting Tax Revenue Séries for Discretionary Changes" (unpublished, International Monetary Fund, August 14, 1974.
9. Choudhry, Nurun N., "A Study of the Elasticity of the West Malaysian Income Tax System, 1961-70", IMF Staff Papers, Vol. XXII, 1975.
10. Dwivedi, D.N., "Elasticities and Buoyancy of Excise Taxation in India", *Indian Economic Review*, No. 2 October, 1976.
11. Govinda Rao, M., "Tax Reform in India: Achievements and Challenges", *Asia – Pasific Development Journal*, Vol. 7, No. 2, December 2000.
12. Gregory C. Chow, "Tests of Equality between sets of Coefficients in two linear Regressions", *Econometrica*, Vol. 28, No. 3, 1960.
13. Mansfield, Charles Y., "Elasticity and Buoyancy of a Tax System: A Method Applied to Paraguay", IMF Staff Papers, Vol. XIX, 1972.

14. Purohit, M.C., "Buoyancy and Income – Elasticity of State taxes in India", *Artha Vijnana*, Vol. 20, No. 5, September, 1978.

15. Rao, V.G., *The Responsiveness of the Indian Tax System 1960-61 to 1973-74*, Allied, 1979.

16. Sahota, G.S., *Indian Tax Structure and Economic Development*, Asia Publishing House, Bombay, 1961.

17. Sahota, G.S., *Indian Tax Structure and Economic Development*, Asia Publishing House, Bombay, 1961.

18. Singer, N.M., "The Use of Dummy Variables in Estimating the Income-Elasticity of State Income Tax Revenues", *National Tax Journal*, Vol. XXI, No. 2, June 1968.

19. Sury, M.M., "Elasticity of Tax Revenue: Some Measurement Problems", *The Indian Economic Journal*, Vol. 26, 1978.

20. Upender, M., "An Income Tax Laffer curve: the Indian Experience", *Artha Vijnana,* Vol. XLI, N. 2, June 1999.

21. Upender, M., *Estimates of coefficients of Economic Relationships*, (2002), Manak Publications, New Delhi.

22. Gregory C. Chow, "Tests of Equality between sets of Coefficients in two linear Regressions", *Econometrica*, Vol. 28, No. 3, 1960.

6

Wage Rate Elasticity of Labour

1. Need for Empirical Study

The empirical information on the estimates of the wage rate elasticity of labour productivity in the major Indian industries is indispensable in order to take appropriate decisions with regard to substitution possibilities between inputs. So far as the empirical information on the estimates of the wage rate elasticity of labour productivity which is the elasticity of substitution between labour and capital is concerned a good number of empirical studies (Asif Banarji [1975], Goldar [1986], Gujarati [1966], Isher Judge Ahulwalia [1981], Sinha and Sawhney [1970], Upender [1996], Diwan and Gujarati [1968], Mehta [1980], Swamy [1984], Shankar [1970], Umar Kazi [1980] Vijay Basin and Vijay Seth 1977], Sanjib Pohit, Rajesh Chadha, Bina and Sangeeta [1996], and Inderpal Kaur [1997]) have been carried out on the basis of time series annual data. Barely a single cross sectional study on the degree of elasticity of substitution between labour and capital, the wage rate elasticity of labour productivity, in twenty eight Indian Industries was carried out by Damodar Gujarati for the year 1958 by estimating a Constant Elasticity of Substitution production function. Therefore there is a need to provide empirical information on the estimate of the wage rate elasticity of labour productivity to know the extent of substitution possibilities between labour and capital across the major Industries [Factory Sector] in India using latest cross section data. Keeping this in view, an attempt has been made in the present paper to provide empirical content to the wage rate elasticity of labour productivity across the major industries at a point of time [for latest year] by using latest cross section data available for the year 2007-08.

2. Empirical Methodology

2.1: Cross Section Data

The required cross section data on Net Value Added, Gross Output [Production], Total Persons Engaged, Workers [Labour], Total Emoluments and Wages to Workers [Wages] for the twenty six major Indian Industry group for the year 2007-2008 has been collected from the Annual Survey of Industries [Factory Sector] 2007- 08. The net value added and Gross Output have been deflated by the whole sale price index [WPI] for manufactured products and total emoluments and wages have been deflated by the consumer price index [CPI] for industrial workers to convert the series into real variables. The whole sale price index for manufactured products and consumer price index for industrial workers for 2007-08 have been collected from the Economic Survey 2009-10.

2.2: Variables Used

[i] Production [P]: Net Value Added and Gross Output have been considered as proxy for Production.

[ii] Wages [W]: Total Emoluments and wages to workers have been considered as proxy for wages.

[iii] Labour [L]: Total Persons Engaged and workers have been considered as labour in the present study.

*[iv] Labour Productivity [P/L*1/WPI]* = Real Net Value Added or Gross Output [proxy for Production] per unit of labour.

*[v] Wage Rate [W/L*1/CPI]* = Real wage per unit of labour.

2.3: Empirical Model for estimation the wage rate elasticity of labour productivity

With a view to estimate the wage rate elasticity of labour productivity to know the extent of substitution possibilities between the labour and capital across the major Indian Industries for year 2007-08, the following constant elasticity of substitution production function has been fitted to the cross section data generated. The specification of the constant elasticity of substitution [CES] production function is

$$P = A\ [\delta K^{-\rho} + (1-\delta)\ L^{-\rho}]^{-1/\rho} \qquad \ldots (1)$$

Where

P = Production [Real Net value added or Gross Output].

K and L = Capital and Labour inputs respectively.

ρ = Extent of substitution between labour and capital related to $\sigma = 1/\ 1+\rho$.

δ = Distribution parameter.

The above equation has been estimated empirically by OLS method under the marginal productivity conditions [marginal productivity of labour = real wage rate]. The marginal product of labour [MPL] is obtained from the above function [equation -1] as follows:

$$\partial P/\partial L = A[\delta K^{-\rho} + (1-\delta)L^{-\rho}]^{1/\rho}\ [\delta\ K^{-\rho}\ (1-\delta)L^{-\rho}]^{-1}\ (1-\delta)\ L^{(1+\rho)}$$

$$= [P * P^{\rho}]\ /\ A^{\rho}\ [1-\delta].\ 1\ /\ L^{1+\rho}$$

$$= 1-\delta\ /\ A^{\rho} * P^{1+\rho} * 1/\ L^{1+\rho}$$

Equilibrium condition between $\partial P/\partial L$ and W/L*1/CPI [i.e., Marginal Product of labour [MPL] is equal to Real Wage Rate], the most ideal situation that represents the absence of exploitation of the labour, is

MPL = Real Wage Rate

$$\partial P/\partial L = W\ /\ L$$

$$[1-\delta\ /\ A^{\rho}]\ [P\ /\ L]^{1+\rho} = W\ /\ L$$

$$[P/L]^{1+\rho} = [A^{\rho}\ /\ (1-\delta) * W/L]$$

$$[P/L] = [A^{\rho}\ /(1-\delta) * W/L]^{1/1+\rho}$$

$\ln [P/L] = 1/1+\rho \ln[A^{\rho} / 1-\delta] + 1/1+\rho \ln [W/L]$

$1/1+\rho \ln [A^{\rho}/1-\delta] =$ Constant

$1/1+\rho = \sigma =$ wage rate elasticity of labour productivity [Elasticity of Substitution]

$$\ln [P/L] = \text{Constant} + \sigma \ln [W/L] \quad \ldots (2)$$

The coefficient on ln W/L in the above regression of ln P/L on W/L is the estimate of constant elasticity of substitution (σ) between labour ands capital,

$\sigma = 1/1+\rho$

$\rho = (1/\sigma) - 1$

Specification of CES Production function with real variables is

$$\ln [P/L^{*}1/WPI] = \text{Constant} + \sigma \ln [W/L^{*}1/CPI] \quad \ldots (3)$$

Where

P/ L*1/WSPI is the real labour productivity.

P = Production; L = Labour :WPI = Whole sale price index for manufactured product.

W = Wages; CPI = Consumer price index for industrial workers.

The above equation has been estimated under the equilibrium [marginal product of labour = real wage rate] conditions with one way causation between labour productivity and wage rate. The Newey-West method [known as Hetroscedasticity and Autocorrelation consistent, HAC, standard errors] is followed to correct the OLS standard errors for autocorrelation and hetroscedasticity problems.

3. Estimates of wage rate elasticity of labour productivity across the Indian Industries

The regression results of the Constant Elasticity of Substitution Production Function fitted to the cross section data belonging to twenty six major Indian Industries [factory sector] for the year 2007- 08 have been set out in table 6.1.

Table 6.1: Results of the CES Production Function : Wage rate elasticities of of labour productivity across the twenty six major Indian Industries in 2007-08

Specification of the Model	*Constant*	*Constant Wage rate elasticity of labour productivity*	R^2	*Nature of Wage rate elasticity of labour productivity*	*Implication of the elasticity*
I	3.120929 [0.123445] (0.146359)	1.110774 [0.201102] (0.281956)	0.559701	> Unity	Substitution possibilities are skewed in favour of labour in the Indian major Industries.
II	4.146686 [0.165304] (0.216982)	1.624214* [0.230435] (0.335865)	0.574272	> Unity	
III	1.363663 [0.098200] (0.126834)	1.185324* [0.159976] (0.227427)	0.695814	> Unity	
IV	2.406747 [C.132944] (0.205244)	1.669341* [0.185326] (0.265408)	0.771726	> Unity	

Notes:

1. Figures within [ ] show the OLS standard errors.
2. Figures within ( ) show the HAC standard errors.
3. * Significant at one percent level.
4. Model - I : ln [Gross Output /Total persons engaged*1/WPI] =Constant + σ ln [Total Emoluments/ Total persons engaged *1/CPI].
5. Model- II : ln [Gross Output /Workers*1/WPI] =Constant + σ ln [Wages / Workers *1/CPI].
6. Model-III: ln [Net Value Added /Total persons engaged*1/WPI] =Constant + σ ln [Total Emoluments/ Total persons engaged *1/CPI].
7. Model-IV: ln [Net Value Added / Workers*1/WPI] =Constant + σ ln [Wages / Workers*1/CPI].

The regression results based constant elasticity of substitution production function fitted to the cross section data for 2007-08 show that the constant wage rate elasticities of labour productivity across twenty six majour Indian Industries are not only significantly positive but also more than unity ranging from 1.11 to 1.67 in the four models. A one percent increase in real wage rate will lead to increase the labour productivity more than one percent across the major industries in India This empirical information reveals the fact that the substitution possibilities are more in favour of labour across the major Indian industries [factory sector]. In other words the production per unit of wage is found to be increasing with the increase in wage rate across the major industries. This indicates that factor proportions are reasonably responding to the factor price changes across the industries. Therefore there is a need to redirect the labour surplus Indian Economy towards intensive use of labour.

4. Conclusion

The present paper examines the extent of substitution possibilities between labour and capital across twenty six major industries in India during 2007-08 by estimating the constant wage rate elasticities of labour productivity with different variables with the help of constant elasticity of substitution production function under marginal productivity conditions with one way causation between labour productivity and wage rate. The numerical values of wage rate elasticities of labour productivity in four models with different variables are found to be more than unity suggesting the existence of considerable potential for substitution of labour for capital across the major Indian industries. Therefore there is a need to transmit the labour surplus Indian Economy towards intensive use of labour.

References

1. Arrow, H.B., Chenery B.S. Minhas and R.M. Solow, "Capital-Labour Substitution and Economic Efficiency," *The Review of Economics and Statistics*, August 1961.

2. Asif Banarji, *Capital Intensity and Productivity in Indian Industry*, MacMillan Co., New Delhi, 1975.
3. Cobb,CW and Douglas PH, "Theory of production", *American Economic Review*, Vol. XVIII, 1928.
4. Diwan R.K. and D.N. Gujarati, "Employment and Productivity in Indian Industries – Some Questions of the Theory and Policy", *Artha Vijnana*, Vol. 10, No. 1, March, 1968, pp. 29-67.
5. Goldar, B.N., *Productivity Growth in Indian Industry*, Allied, New Delhi, 1986.
6. Gujarati, D.N. "A Test of ACMS Production Function: Indian Industries", 1958, *Indian Journal of Industrial Relations*, Vol. 2, No. 1, 1966, pp. 95-97.
7. Inderpal Kaur, *Impact of Liberalisation on Indian Industry,Deep Publications*, New Delhi, 1997.
8. Isher Judge Ahulwalia, *Productivity Growth in Indian Manufacturing*, Oxford University Press, 1981.
9. Krishna K.L. (Ed.), *Econometric Applications in India*, Oxford University Press, 1997.
10. Mehta, S.S., *Productivity, Production Function and Technical Change – A Survey of Some Indian Industries*, Concept Publishing Co., New Delhi, 1980.
11. Panchamukhi, VR, "A Survey of Econometric Studies in the fields of Production, International Trade and Money and Banking" in A Survey of Research in Economics, Vol. VII, *Econometrics* [ICSSR] Allied, 1978.
12. Sanjib Pohit, Rajesh Chadha, P.L. Bina and N. Sangeeta, "Estimation of Substitution Parameter in Indian Industries", *National Council of Applied Economic Research*, New Delhi, 1996.
13. Shankar, U. Elasticities of Substitution and Returns to Scale in Indian Manufacturing Industries, *International Economic Review*, Vol. II, No. 3, October 1970, pp. 399-411.
14. Sinha J.N. and P.K. Sawhney, *Wages and Productivity in Selected Indian Industries*, Vikas Publications, 1970.
15. Swamy, T.L.N. "Factor Substitution in Indian Industries: Some Cross-Section Evidence", *Margin*, January 1984, pp. 31-38.

16. Umar, A. Kazi, The VES Production Function: A Case Study for Indian Manufacturing Industries, Oxford Economic Papers, Vol. 32, No. 1, March, 1980, pp. 163-75.

17. Upender, M., Elasticity of Labour Productivity in Indian Manufacturing Sector", *Economic and Political Weekly,* Vol. XXXI, No. 21, May 25, 1996, pp. M7-M10.

18. Upender, M. *Estimates of coefficients of Economic Relationships*, Manak Publications, New Delhi, 2002.

19. Vijay, K. Basin and Vijay K. Seth, "Estimation of Production Functions for Indian Manufacturing Sector", *Artha Vignana*, Vol. 19, No. 2, June 1977, pp. 113-28.

7

Effectiveness of Income Tax Laffer Curve*

1. Introduction

Thesis of the Laffer curve

One of the recommendations of the Tax Reform Committee [1991] was that in order to make the country's direct tax system more effective it was necessary that the income tax regime must have lower rates of taxation. This recommendation seems to be influenced by the laffer effect or laffer curve. The empirical validity of income tax laffer curve[1] has been getting a lot of attention in the Indian Tax System in view of the substantial reductions in maximum marginal tax rates from 50 per cent to 40 per cent and from 40 per cent to 30 per cent to raise the revenue from income tax. The bell shaped laffer curve [Fig. 7.1] shows the relationship between tax rates and government revenues[2]. This curve has two regions. The first region is concerned with the positive relationship[3] and the second region is concerned with the negative relationship[4] between personal income tax rates [mmtr] and tax revenues [rit]. As tax rates rise from zero [Points a, b, c and d], revenue increases until the optimum point [e] is reached. This is

*Reproduced from the *Indian Economic Journal*, Vol. 49, No. 4, 2001.

known as the normal range of laffer curve. If the tax rates are increased further [Points f, g, h and i on the laffer curve shown by shaded area] then the government revenue falls. This is known as the prohibitive range of laffer curve. It should be prominent to note that so far as the relationship between the revenue from income tax and tax rates is concerned that the prohibitive range of the laffer curve, despite the fact that there is an inverse relationship between them, has two facets. One is concerned with the increase in the revenue from income tax by reducing the tax rates, which is affordable, and other is concerned with the decrease in the revenue by increasing the tax rates, which is unaffordable. The argument that the laffer curve phenomenon works in India stands valid, if the impact of reductions in tax rate on raising income tax revenue is found to be *more effective* for all the financial years from 1993 to 2001. *Was the laffer curve phenomenon working effectively in India?* This needs an empirical verification. The present diminutive exercise is an attempt, *inter alia*, to provide empirical evidence to this query.

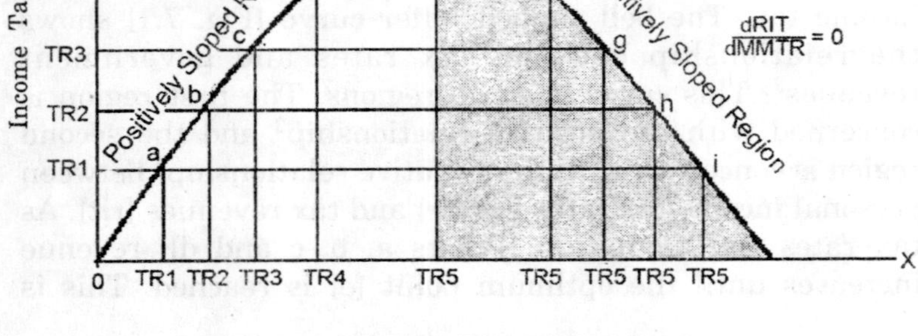

Fig. 7.1 : Income Tax Laffer Curve.

2. Empirical Studies on the Validity of Laffer Curve in India during post tax reform period

There were two empirical studies on the validity of the laffer curve for the Indian Economy during post tax reform period. Pinaki Chakraborthy[5] in his paper examined to see whether the lowering of tax rates resulted in higher tax mobilisation. The period covered in this study was from 1990-91 to 1997-98. The analysis of year-to-year movement of income tax rate and collections brings out that tax rate reduction in a particular year did not result in an improvement in elasticity in that year itself. In fact, elasticity seems to decline with rate reduction. If the improvement in elasticity was due to the reduction in tax rate, it was registered only after a time lag of at least one year [t-1] incase of income tax. The movement of tax rates and income elasticities showed that generally reduction in tax rate can not make a tax more buoyant instantly. There was a time lag involved. Since there was a time lag, the expectation that the laffer curve phenomenon, though not in its purest form, will start operating instantaneously with a reduction in tax rate may well prove far too optimistic. The magnitude of elasticity of income tax revenue with respect to maximum marginal tax rate was not empirically examined in this paper. Upender[6] in his diminutive exercise examined to know whether the Indian Economy was on the downward sloping portion of the laffer curve during the post tax reform period 1992-93 to 1996-97. The year wise estimates of elasticities of income tax revenue with respect to maximum marginal tax rates were found to be persistently negative on account of reduction from 50 per cent to 40 per cent in tax rates confirming the validity of the thesis of negatively sloped region of the laffer curve in India. The effectiveness of the prohibitive range of the laffer curve was not examined in this paper. As the empirical evidence on the presence/ absence of income tax laffer curve in India during 1992-93 to 2000 – 01 is required to know the effort of government in raising the revenue from income tax on account of the reductions in the tax rates from 50 per cent to 40 per cent in the initial phase and from 40 per cent to 30 per cent in the later phase in the context of tax reforms undertaken in India as a key component of the structural adjustment programme, the present exercise was carried out covering the data available till date. This paper will be an enhancement over the above two papers in testing the following.

1. The empirical validity of income tax laffer curve in its precise form during 1961 – 2001 in terms of plotting graph and estimating quadratic equation.
2. the validity of effectiveness of the prohibitive range of the laffer curve on account of downward revision of tax rates during post tax reform period in terms of estimates of tax rate elasticities of income tax revenue and
3. the presence/absence of association between year to year data points of tax buoyancy and elasticity of income tax revenue with respect to maximum marginal tax rates in terms of graph and summary statistic. More specifically the present paper tries to provide the empirical evidence to the following queries:
   (i) Was the income tax laffer curve working in its precise form in India during 1960-61 to 2000 - 01? If not,
   (ii) Was the Indian tax system operating in the prohibitive / normal range of the income laffer curve during post tax reform period? If so, Was it more / less effective?
   (iii) Was Income tax system in India less/more buoyant during post tax reform period? and
   (iv) Was there any association between the points of elasticity of income tax revenue with respect to maximum marginal tax rate and income tax buoyancy ?

3. Method of Analysis and Data

The following form of regression equation was fitted to

the data points covering the period from 1960-61 to 2000-2001 to search the answer for the first query

$RIT = \beta_0+\beta_1 GDP+\beta_2 T+\beta_3 MMTR+\beta_4 MMTR^2 + error$ . . . (1)

Where $\beta_1 > 0$; $\beta_2 > 0$; $\beta_3 < 0$; and $\beta_4 < 0$

RIT= Income Tax Revenue [Rupees crore]

GDP= Gross Domestic Product at Market Prices

T= Time [Years] from 1961 to 2001

MMTR= Maximum Marginal Tax Rate [Per cent]

$MMTR^2$= Square of Maximum Marginal Tax Rate

Both linear [Eq. 2] and double log [Eq. 3] forms of equations were fitted to the data points for post tax reform period to search the answer to the second query. The regression results based on double log form of the equation was retained for the analysis on the grounds that goodness of fit and the constant elasticity of RIT with respect to the reductions in MMTR. It should also be noted that the sign of the regression coefficients of MMTR in the linear and ln MMTR in the double log models were found to be negative.

$RIT = \beta_0 + \beta_1 MMTR + error$ . . . (2)

Where β_1 [7] [rate of response of RIT per a unit change in MMTR, Which was constant,

d RIT/ d MMTR] < 0 signifies the prohibitive range of the laffer curve during post tax reform period

$\ln RIT = \beta_0 + \beta_1 \ln MMTR + error$ . . . (3)

Where β1[8] [percent response of RIT to the changes (reductions) in MMTR ($E_{RIT.MMTR}$)], which was constant, d ln RIT/d ln MMTR] < 0 also signifies the prohibitive range of the laffer curve during post tax reform period. If the size of the regression coefficient of ln mmtr [absolute value], β_1, is less than unity, then the impact of reductions in the maximum marginal tax rate on raising the income tax revenue will, on the average, be less effective[9] [inelastic nature] in the prohibitive range of the laffer curve during post tax reform period ; If the size of the regression coefficient of ln mmtr, β_1, is more than unity, then the impact of reductions in the maximum marginal tax rate on raising the income tax revenue will, on the average, be more effective[10] [elastic nature] in the prohibitive range of the laffer curve during post tax reform period. As the summary statistic gives, on the average, the magnitude of elasticity of income tax revenue with respect to tax rates on during post tax reform period, the year to year estimates of the elasticities of income tax revenue with respect to maximum marginal tax rates were also worked out to examine the impact of reductions in tax rate from 50 per cent to 40 per cent on raising the income tax revenue by taking the ratio of proportionate change in income tax revenue to the proportionate change in maximum marginal tax rate. The tax rate elasticities for the years 1992-93, 1993-94, 1994-95,1995-96 and 1996-97 were calculated as follows:

$$E_{RIT.MMTR\ 1992\text{-}93} = (RIT_{1992\text{-}93} - RIT_{1991\text{-}92} / RIT_{1991\text{-}92}) / (MMTR_{1992\text{-}93} - MMTR_{1991\text{-}92} / MMTR_{1991\text{-}92})$$

$$E_{RIT.MMTR1993\text{-}94} = (RIT_{1993\text{-}94} - RIT_{1992\text{-}93} / RIT_{1992\text{-}93}) / (MMTR_{1993\text{-}94} - MMTR_{1991\text{-}92} / MMTR_{1991\text{-}92})$$

$$E_{RIT.MMTR1994\text{-}95} = (RIT_{1994\text{-}95} - RIT_{1993\text{-}94} / RIT_{1993\text{-}94}) / (MMTR_{1994\text{-}95} - MMTR_{1991\text{-}92} / MMTR_{1991\text{-}92})$$

$$E_{RIT.MMTR1995\text{-}96} = (RIT_{1995\text{-}96} - RIT_{1994\text{-}95} / RIT_{1994\text{-}95}) / (MMTR_{1995\text{-}96} - MMTR_{1991\text{-}92} / MMTR_{1991\text{-}92})$$

$$E_{RIT.MMTR1996\text{-}97} = (RIT_{1996\text{-}97} - RIT_{1995\text{-}96} / RIT_{1995\text{-}96}) / (MMTR_{1996\text{-}97} - MMTR_{1991\text{-}92} / MMTR_{1991\text{-}92})$$

The proportionate change in maximum marginal tax rate was constant during 1992-93 to 1996-97 as the maximum marginal tax rate reduced from 50% in 1991-92 to 40% in 1992-93, which was retained till 1996-97.

In order to examine the impact of reductions in tax rate from 40 per cent to 30% per cent on raising the income tax revenue, the tax rate elasticities for the years 1997-98,

1998-99, 1999-00 and 2000-01 were also calculated as follows:

$$E_{RIT.MMTR1997\text{-}98} = (RIT_{1997\text{-}98} - RIT_{1996\text{-}97} / RIT_{1996\text{-}97}) / (MMTR_{1997\text{-}98} - MMTR_{1996\text{-}97} / MMTR_{1996\text{-}97})$$

$$E_{RIT.MMTR1998\text{-}99} = (RIT_{1998\text{-}99} - RIT_{1997\text{-}98} / RIT_{1997\text{-}98}) / (MMTR_{1998\text{-}99} - MMTR_{1997\text{-}98} / MMTR_{1997\text{-}98})$$

$$E_{RIT.MMTR1999\text{-}00} = (RIT_{1999\text{-}00} - RIT_{1998\text{-}99} / RIT_{1998\text{-}99}) / (MMTR_{1999\text{-}00} - MMTR_{1998\text{-}99} / MMTR_{1998\text{-}99})$$

$$E_{RIT.MMTR2000\text{-}01} = (RIT_{2000\text{-}01} - RIT_{1999\text{-}00} / RIT_{1999\text{-}00}) / (MMTR_{2000\text{-}01} - MMTR_{1999\text{-}00} / MMTR_{1999\text{-}00})$$

The proportionate change in maximum marginal tax rate was constant during 1997-98 to 2000-01 as the maximum marginal tax rate reduced from 40% in 1996-97 to 30% in 1997 - 98 which was retained till 2000-2001. Thus it is clear that time lag[11] was continuously involved in estimating these elasticities $[E_{RIT.MMTR}]$.

To examine whether the income tax system in India was more / less buoyant during post tax reform period, the following form of double - log equation[12] was fitted to the data points.

$$\ln RIT = \beta_0 + \beta_1 \ln GDP + error \quad \ldots (4)$$

Where $\beta_1 = \ln d\ RIT / \ln d\ GDP$ [the constant estimate of income tax buoyancy] > 0.

If β_1 is less than unity then the income tax system will, on the average, be less buoyant[13] : If β_1 is more than unity then the income tax system will, on the average, be more buoyant[14]. As the summary statistic gives, on the average, the magnitude of the tax buoyancy during post tax reform period, the year-to-year tax buoyancy estimates were also calculated. The degree of association between the year to year estimates of tax buoyancy and elasticity of income tax revenue with respect to national income, though the relationship between them was not yet theoretically established in the literature of public finance, was also worked out to provide an empirical content by a simple correlation coefficient.[15] The year to year estimates of income tax buoyancy [$E_{RIT.GDP}$] were worked out for the years 1992-93 to 2000 – 01 by taking the ratio of the proportionate change in income tax revenue to the proportionate change in national income as follows:

$$E_{RIT.GDP} = (RIT_1 - RIT_{t-1} / IT_{t-1}) / GDP_t - GDP_{t-1} / DP_{t-1})$$

The required data on Income tax revenue [RIT], maximum marginal tax rate [MMTR] and gross domestic product [GDP] at current market prices were collected from the Economic Survey –2000-01[16], different documents of the Indian Public Finance Statistics[17], Economic and Political Weekly[18], and Public Finance [CMIE][19]. The data collected on gdp and income tax revenue for the period from 1961 to 1999 were realised [actual] while for the years 1999-2000 and 2000-2001 were revised and budget estimates respectively. The results of the analysis will be subjected to the data used.

4. Analysis of the Results

The estimates of the regression coefficients of the gdp, time, maximum marginal tax rate and square of it [not reported here], based on time series data[20] [Equation 1] show that the signs of the estimates of coefficients of mmtr and $mmtr^2$ were positive and negative respectively but insignificant. The sign of the coefficient of time was significantly negative, which was not conceivable. The sign of the regression coefficient of gdp was significantly positive. Further, the values of R^2 and Adj.R^2 were very high, which might be due to the presence of multicollinearity[21] among the mmtr, $mmtr^2$, trend and gdp. Therefore, without the intercept, the following form of equation with the two necessary independent variables mmtr and its square, was also fitted to the data points to verify the robustness of the income tax laffer curve during 1961-2001

$$RIT = \beta_1 MMTR + \beta_2 MMTR^2 + \text{error} \qquad \ldots (1a)$$

$$\beta_1 > 0 : \beta_2 < 0$$

d RIT/d MMTR [the rate of change in RIT with respect to MMTR][22]= $\beta_1 - 2\ \beta_2$ MMTR

d^2 RIT/d $MMTR^2$ [the rate of change of d RIT/d MMTR][23] = $- 2\beta_2 < 0$

The estimates of regression coefficients of mmtr and $mmtr^2$ are furnished in table 7.1.

Table 7.1: Income Tax Revenue Function-Results of Regression Analysis

Dependent Variable: RIT			
Method: Least Squares			
Sample: 1961 2001			
Included observations: 41			
Variable	*Coefficient*	*Std. Error*	*t-Statistic*
MMTR*	417.2061	82.83602	5.036530
$MMTR^2$*	-5.533310	1.260645	-4.389268
R-squared	0.180094		
Adjusted R-squared	0.159070		
F-statistic	8.566400		
Durbin-Watson stat	0.105045		

Note: * Significant at 1 % level.

So far as income tax revenue and its relationship with the maximum marginal tax rate was concerned, the sign of coefficient of marginal maximum tax rate turned out positively and that of its square negatively significant* confirming that, though the shape of the income tax curve was not precisely in line with the bell shaped laffer curve, a sort of income tax curve [Fig. 7.2] withnormal range and prohibitive range evincing that there was a point at which the revenue from income tax can be maximised at a specific rate of income tax, *all else equal*. But mmtr and $mmtr^2$ together could not be able to explain larger proportion of total variation in rit as the values of R^2 adj. R^2 were found to be very low signifying that overall goodness fit of the model [Equation 1a] was low.

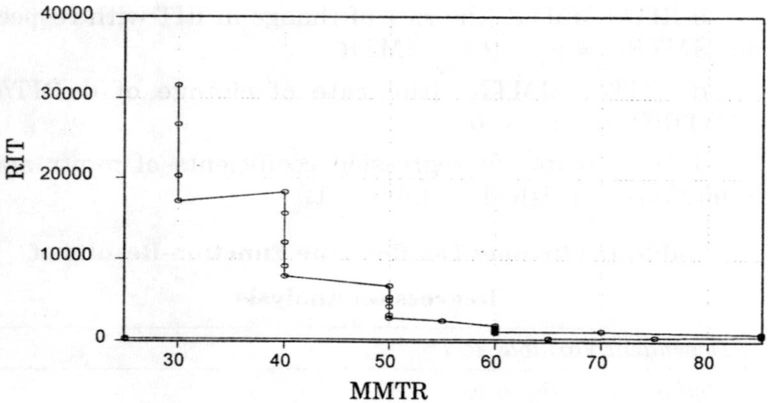

Fig. 7.2. Income Tax Revenue (RIT) – Tax Rate (MMTR)

Therefore it is indispensable to observe was there, at least, a noteworthy negative relationship between maximum marginal tax rate and income tax revenue during post tax reform period. Further, the intention of this exercise was to check up the impact of the proportionate reduction in maximum marginal tax rate on the proportionate increase in the revenue from income tax during post tax reform period. For this purpose the double - log regression relation [Equation 3][24] was fitted to the post tax reform period

Table 7.2: Income Tax Revenue Function – Results of Regression Analysis

Dependent Variable: LOG(RIT)			
Method: Least Squares			
Sample: 1992 2001			
Included observations: 10			
Variable	*Coefficient*	*Std. Error*	*t-Statistic*
Constant	18.12514	1.994034	9.089689
LOG(MMTR)*	-2.371192	0.553865	-4.281176
R-squared	0.696146		
F-statistic	18.32846		
Durbin-Watson stat	1.405900		

Note: * Significant at 5 % level.

data to examine the impact of substantial reductions in the maximum marginal tax rate from 50 percent in 1991-92 to 40 percent in 1992-93 and from 40 percent to 30 percent in 1997-98 on the revenue from income tax. The estimate of the regression coefficient of maximum marginal tax rate is furnished in table 7.2.

The results exemplify that the regression coefficient of maximum marginal tax rate of personal income tax, which was the constant elasticity of revenue from income tax with respect to maximum marginal tax rate, was not only significantly negative but also more than unity showing that during the period under consideration, on the average, a one percent slash in maximum marginal tax rate induced to augment the revenue from income tax by more than two percent. This corroborates that the Indian economy was operating in the prohibitive range of the income tax laffer curve during post tax reform period. The negative relationship between mmtr and rit can also be observed in Fig. 7.3. The MMTR and RIT were moving in the opposite direction in all the years during post tax reform period except for the year 1997-98 where they were in the same direction**.

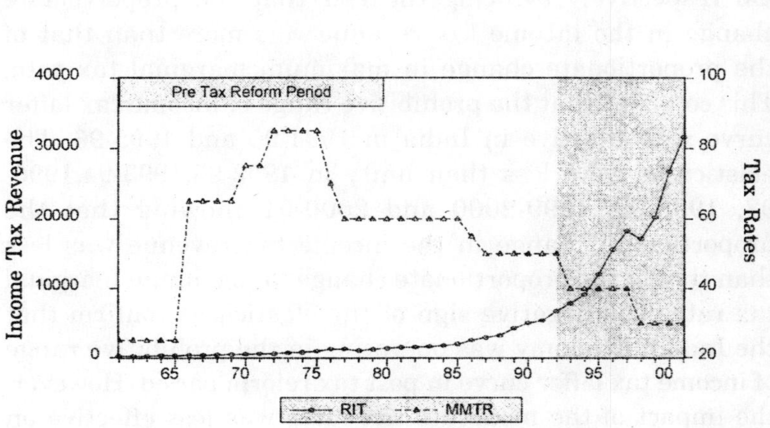

Fig. 7.3. Movements in Income Taxc Revenue (RIT) and Tax Rates (MMTR).

It can also be inferred from the observed constant elasticity of income tax revenue with respect to maximum marginal tax rate that the growth rate of income tax revenue was positive [16.75%][25] while the growth rate of maximum marginal tax rate was negative [- 6.35%][26] during post tax reform period. As the summary statistic gives on the average the elasticity of income tax revenue with respect to maximum marginal tax rate during post tax reform period, the year-to-year elasticities were also considered. The impact of the substantial reductions [by 10 per cent] in maximum marginal tax rate from 50 percent in 1991-92 to 40 percent in 1992-93 and from 40 percent in 1996-97 to 30 per cent in 1998 – 99 on the revenue from income tax was examined in terms of year-to-year elasticities of maximum marginal tax rate of income tax revenue for the years from 1992-93 to 2000-01. The size/magnitude and sign of year to year estimates of elasticities of maximum marginal tax rate of income tax revenue are furnished in table 7.3. The numerical values illustrate that these elasticities were negative in all the financial years of post tax reform period and more than unity only in the years 1994-95 and 1995 -96 respectively evincing the fact that the proportionate change in the income tax revenue was more than that of the proportionate change in maximum marginal tax rate. This confirms that the prohibitive range of income tax laffer curve was effective in India in 1994-95 and 1995-96. The elasticities were less than unity in 1992-93,1993-94,1996-97, 1998-99, 1999-2000 and 2000-01 showing that the proportionate change in the income tax revenue was less than that of the proportionate change in maximum marginal tax rate. The negative sign of the elasticities confirm that the Indian Economy was operating in the prohibitive range of income tax laffer curve in post tax reform period. However, the impact of the moderate tax rates was less effective on augmenting the income tax revenue in 1992-93, 1993-94, 1996-97, 1999-2000 and 2000-01 as the tax rate elasticities were found to be less than unity. Mere operating in the prohibitive range of income tax laffer curve was not sufficient during the post tax reform period The impact of reductions in tax rates by 10 per cent on raising income tax revenue was more effective in 1994-95 and 1995-96 respectively as the tax rate elasticities exceeded unity. The bewildering aspect is that the elasticity of maximum marginal tax rate of income tax revenue was positive and less than unity in 1997-98 showing the nonexistence of prohibitive range of the income tax laffer curve in that year. The sign of the proportionate change in income tax revenue was negative in 1997-98 showing that the revenue from income tax fell in 1998 as compared to the revenue in 1997. *This shortfall could be because of the diversion of the funds into VDIS*. The positive elasticity of mmtr of income tax revenue implies that a one percent reduction in tax rate reduced the income tax revenue by 0.16 percent. Thus, so far as income tax revenue and its relationship with maximum marginal tax rate was concerned, the laffer curve phenomenon in terms of an inverse relationship [prohibitive range] did not work in this year. It should be noted that after the announcement of reductions in maximum marginal tax rates from 50 per cent in 1991-92 to 40 per cent in 1992-93 and from 40 per cent in 1996-97 to 30 per cent in 1998-99, despite the fact that the number of tax returns filed by the individuals increased from 4322804 in 1992-93 *{Figures within the brackets against each year show the number of income tax returns filed: 1993-94 [4874440], 1994-95 [6717453], 1995-96 [6786781], 1996-97 [7357548]}* to 9049398 in 1997-98 [This is the most recent year for which official data are available on number of returns filed: *Public Finance Statistics 2000-01*, Government of India, p. 77] showing an increase of 109% in 1998-99 as compared to 1992-93, the size of income tax rate elasticity did not ascend incessantly. The constant elasticity of the number of tax returns filed by individuals with respect to the maximum marginal tax rate was significantly negative and more than unity [-1.7147 whose t value was – 2.93861] showing on the average that a one percent reduction in mmtr increased the number of tax returns filed by more than one percent. It should also be noted while addressing a meeting of the advisory committee of the central board of direct taxes the union finance minister said the Government was firm in doubling the number of tax payers in the next four years as the current number of assessees was still a small proportion of the population and the revenue department would step up the scrutiny of the filed income tax returns in order to plug tax evasion and augment the revenue collections [*The Hindu*, dated 23.11.2001]. Will the size of income tax buoyancy and tax rate elasticity of income tax be improved if the number of tax payers is doubled in the next four years? It should also be noted that the parliamentary standing committee in its report presented to parliament has strongly indicted the union finance ministry by saying that "the persistent shortfalls despite the steep downward revision of budgetary estimates at the revised estimates stage confirm the fact that the finance ministry has been myopic in its assumptions and the parameters have been selected without weighing the pros and cons of the existing economic scenario in detail and assessing the levels of tax buoyancy. Such continuous shortfall in actual receipts over budget estimates reduces the credibility of the budget preparing institution in particular and finance ministry in general." The revenue department had not evolved any structural mechanism to identify those income tax officers who were resorting to under-assessment and contributing to shortfall, the report said. [The Hindu, dated 26-05-2002] The year-to-year movements in the size/magnitude of tax rate elasticities with respect to the maximum marginal tax rates from 1993 to 2001 can be observed in Fig. 7.4.

Table 7.3: Movements in maximum marginal tax rate elasticities of Revenue from income tax

Financial year	*Maximum marginal tax rate (%)*	*Finan-cial year*	*Tax rate elasticities of income tax revenue*	*Nature of elasticity*
1992-93	40	1993	-0.859456	Less than unity
1993-94	40	1994	-0.782835	Less than unity
1994-95	40	1995	-1.590486	More than unity
1995-96	40	1996	-1.483160	More than unity
1996-97	40	1997	-0.846267	Less than unity
1997-98	30	1998	0.155504	Less than unity
1998-99	30	1999	-0.458852	Less than unity
1999-00	30	2000	-0.796763	Less than unity
2000-01	30	2001	-0.459639	Less than unity

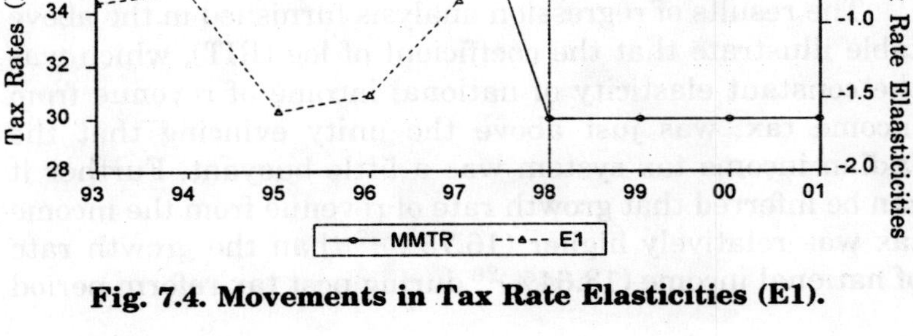

Fig. 7.4. Movements in Tax Rate Elasticities (E1).

In order to see the degree of association between the year to year estimates of tax rate elasticities and income tax buoyancy during post tax reform period, the year to year estimates of income tax buoyancy and summary statistic of constant income tax buoyancy [the impact of national income on income tax revenue] were worked out. For this purpose the double log form of equation [Eq. 4] was fitted to the data points during post tax reform period. The estimate of regression coefficient of ln GDP is furnished in table 7.4.

Table 7.4: Estimate of Income Tax Buoyancy – Results of Regression Results

Dependent Variable: LOG(RIT)			
Method: Least Squares			
Sample: 1992 2001			
Included observations: 10			
Variable	*Coefficient*	*Std. Error*	*t-Statistic*
Constant	-7.636553	0.906091	-8.428021
LOG(GDP)*	1.229107	0.064594	19.02829
R-squared	0.978383		
F-statistic	362.0759		
Durbin-Watson stat	1.383637		

Note: * Significant at 1% level.

The results of regression analysis furnished in the above table illustrate that the coefficient of log (RIT), which was the constant elasticity of national income of revenue from income tax, was just above the unity evincing that the Indian income tax system was a little buoyant. Further it can be inferred that growth rate of revenue from the income tax was relatively higher (16.75%)[27] than the growth rate of national income (13.64%)[28] during post tax reform period

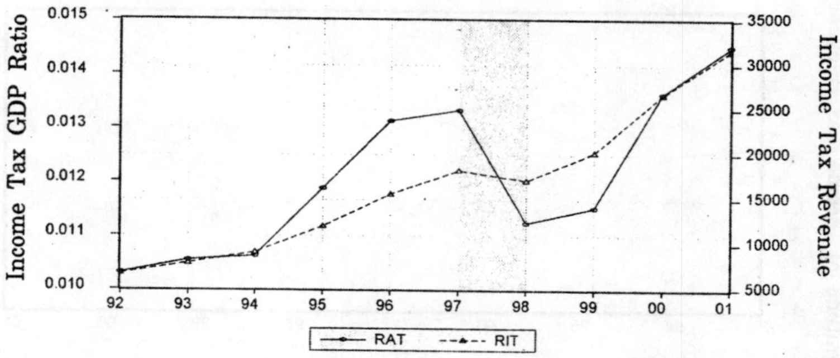

Fig. 7.5. Income Tax GDP Ratio (RAT) and Income Tax Revenue (RTI).

evincing the fact that the ratio of rit to GDP[29] was slightly mounting with the increase in the GDP [Fig. 4.5].

As the summary statistic on the average gives the magnitude of income tax buoyancy during post tax reform period, the year-to-year estimates were also considered. The year to year estimates of income tax buoyancy for the years 1992 to 2001 furnished in table 7.5 show that the size/ magnitude of the elasticity was more than unity in the years 1992, 1995, 1996, 2000 and 2001, while it was around unity in 1993, 1994, 1997 and 1999. The numerical value of the tax buoyancy was positive and more than two in 2000 evincing the fact that the proportionate increase in the income tax revenue was twice than that of the proportionate increase in the gross domestic income. The bewildering aspect is that the size of tax buoyancy was negative and less than unity in 1998 showing that the proportionate change in revenue from income tax was negative and the proportionate change in the income was positive. The size of tax buoyancy was found to be either unity or more than unity in all the years of the post tax reform period except for the year 1997-98 in which it was negative and less than unity showing an inverse association between the income tax revenue and income [Fig. 7.6].

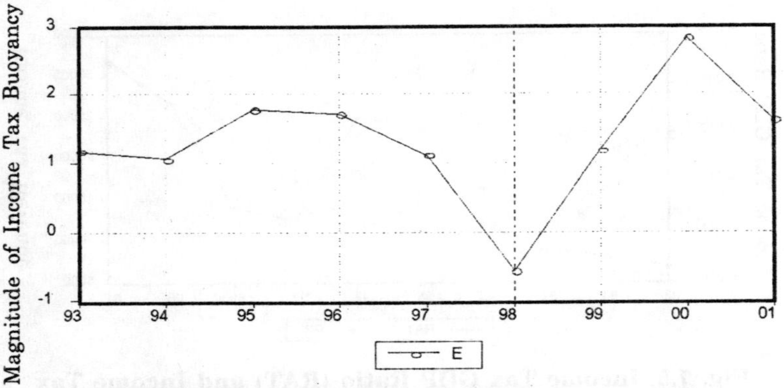

Fig. 7.6. Movements in Income Tax Buoyancy (E).

Table 7.5: Year-to-Year Movements in the Magnitude of Income Tax Buoyancy

Financial Year	*Income Tax Buoyancy*
1991-92	**1.705232**
1992-93	**1.178636**
1993-94	**1.056981**
1994-95	**1.779977**
1995-96	**1.714315**
1996-97	**1.115869**
1997-98	**-0.551795**
1998-99	**1.184855**
1999-00	**2.819892**
2000-01	**1.627037**

Table 7.6: Degree of Association between the year-to-year points of tax rate elasticities and income tax buoyancy

Financial Year	*Tax buoyancy*	*Magnitude of tax buoyancy*	*Tax rate elasticity*	*Magnitude of tax rate elasticity*	*Maximum marginal tax rate (%)*	*Range of the laffer curve*
1992-93	1.178636	= 1	-0.859456	< 1	40	Prohibitive**
1993-94	1.056981	= 1	-0.782835	< 1	40	Prohibitive**
1994-95	1.779977	> 1	-1.590486	> 1	40	Prohibitive*
1995-96	1.714315	> 1	-1.483160	> 1	40	Prohibitive*
1996-97	1.115869	= 1	-0.846267	< 1	40	Prohibitive**
1997-98	-0.551795	< 1	0.155504	< 1	30	Normal
1998-99	1.184855	= 1	-0.458852	< 1	30	Prohibitive**
1999-00	2.819892	> 1	-0.796763	< 1	30	Prohibitive**
2000-01	1.627037	> 1	-0.459639	< 1	30	Prohibitive**

Note: *Effective and **less effective respectively.

With a view to supply an empirical content on the direction and degree of correlation between year to year estimates of income tax buoyancy and the elasticities of income tax revenue with respect to maximum marginal tax rate [Table 7.6], albeit the relationship between them was not yet theoretically established in the literature of public finance, the simple correlation coefficient was calculated. The value of the estimate turned out was - 0.6209 evincing that there subsists negative and high correlation between these two types of elasticities [Fig. 7.6] during post tax reform period in India.

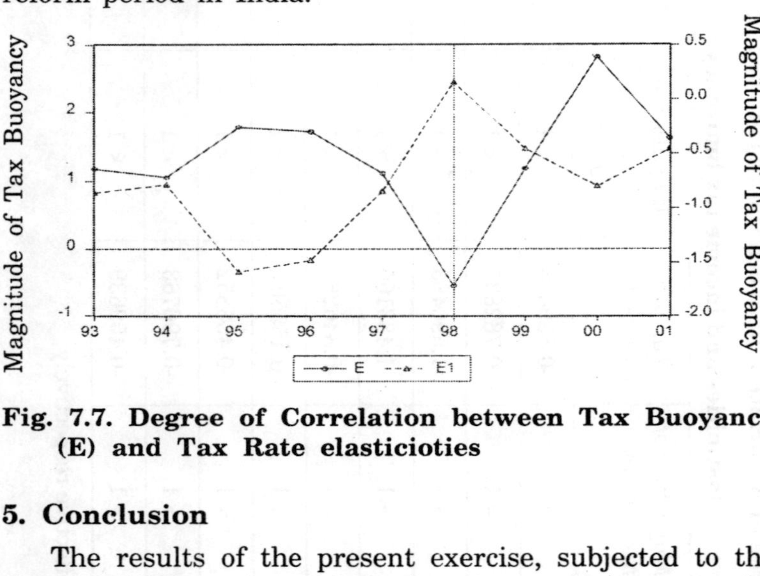

Fig. 7.7. Degree of Correlation between Tax Buoyancy (E) and Tax Rate elasticioties

5. Conclusion

The results of the present exercise, subjected to the data used, show that the year-to-year movements in the negative elasticities of income tax revenue with respect to marginal maximum tax rates confirming that the Indian Income Tax System was operating in the prohibitive range of the laffer curve, though not effective, in all the years of post tax reform period except for the year 1997-98 so far as income tax revenue and its relationship with maximum marginal tax rate was concerned. The argument that the laffer effect works effectively in India will be valid, only if the size of the negative elasticity of income tax revenue with respect to maximum marginal tax rate 30 exceeds unity, which was indeed not apparent in all the financial years of post tax reform period raising a little qualm about the success of tax reforms.

Notes

1. The relationship between tax rate and tax revenue popularised by the American Economist Prof Arthur Laffer. His original work (1975) Published in "The Economics of the Tax Revolt: A Reader (1979)" Arthur B Laffer and Jan P Seymour (Ed) Harcount, New York and "People don't work to pay Tax", Arther B. Laffer Debates with George Perry" Span, November, 1981.

   "Has the Laffer Curve Flattened Out?" Editorial Article, Forbes, November 27, 1989.

   Gene Epstein, "Supply - Side: Past a Point, Reality Negates the Theory" Forbes, March 9, 1998.

   "Laffer Curve" Newsweek, June 26, 1978.

2. This kind of relationship between tax rate and tax revenue will be studied by fitting the following form of quadratic equation without intercept.

   Income Tax Revenue [RIT] = β_1Tax Rate – β_2 (Tax Rate)^2. This equation is mathematically derived for empirical estimation of the laffer curve as follows. Tax revenue[rit] is equal to the tax rate [mmtr] times the base [b] i.e., rit = mmtr*b . . . (1)

   An inverse relationship, which is assumed to be linear, between mmtr and b can be expressed as follows

   $b = \beta_1\beta_2$ mmtr . . . (2)

   Substituting the equation [2] into equation [1] then the following equation will be obtained

   rit = mmtr [β_1–β_2 mmtr] = $\beta_1$mmtr β_2 mmtr^2 . . . (3)

   Thus the empirical estimation of the laffer curve is based on equation [3]. If the intercept is included in the equation [3], then the form of equation will be as follows:

   rit = β_0 + $\beta_1$mmtr – β_2 mmtr^2

3. The derivative of RIT with respect to tax rate = β_1– β_2 [Tax Rate] will be more than zero.

4. The derivative of RIT with respect to tax rate = $\beta_1 - \beta_2$ [Tax Rate] will be less than zero.
5. Pinaki Chakraborthy, (1997) "Tax Reductions and Their Revenue Implications : How Valid Is the Laffer Curve?", *Economic and Political Weekly*, Vol. XVII, No. 36, April 26, pp. 887-90.
6. M Upender, (1999) "An Income Tax Laffer Curve: The Indian Experience", Artha Vijnana, Vol. XLI, No. 2, June, pp. 143-147.
7. The average elasticity of RIT with respect to MMTR [$E_{RIT.MMTR}$], which varies with RIT and MMTR [Variable Elasticity], can also be estimated from the linear regression model, RIT= $\beta_0 + \beta_1$MMTR, [Eq. 2] as follows :

   $E_{RIT.MMTR}$=dRIT / dMMTR* Aeverage of MMTR/Average of RIT = **β_{1*}MMTR / RIT**

   $E_{RIT.MMTR} < 0$ as the sign of β_1 will be negative
8. The rate of response of RIT with respect to MMTR [d RIT / d MMTR], which varies with the values of RIT and MMTR, can be estimated from the double log regression model, ln RIT = $\beta_0 + \beta_1$ ln MMTR [Eq. 3] as follows:

   lndRIT/ dln MMTR = The ratio of dRIT/RIT to dMMTR/ MMTR, which is equal to the ratio of dRIT/dMMTR to MMTR/RIT = β_1

   dRIT/dMMTR = β_{1*}RIT/MMTR
9. The implication of less effectiveness is that the proportionate change/growth rate in RIT will be lower than the proportionate change/growth rate in MMTR.
10. The proportionate change/growth rate in RIT will be higher than the proportionate change/growth rate in MMTR.
11. The impact of reduction in MMTR from 50 per cent [1991-92] to 40 per cent [1992-1997] on RIT is concerned with the time lag [t – 1] as follows:

$$E_{1992\text{-}93} = [RIT_t - RIT_{t-1}/RIT_{t-1}] \;/\; MMTR_t - MMTR_{t-1}/MMTR_{t-1}]$$
$$E_{1993\text{-}94} = [RITt - RIT_{t-1}/RIT_{t-1}] \;/\; MMTR_t - MMTR_{t-2}/MMTR_{t-2}]$$
$$E_{1994\text{-}95} = [RITt - RIT_{t-1}/RIT_{t-1}] \;/\; MMTR_t - MMTR_{t-3}/MMTR_{t-3}]$$
$$E_{1995\text{-}96} = [RITt - RIT_{t-1}/RIT_{t-1}] \;/\; MMTR_t - MMTR_{t-4}/MMTR_{t-4}]$$
$$E_{1996\text{-}97} = [RITt - RIT_{t-1}/RIT_{t-1}] \;/\; MMTR_t - MMTR_{t-5}/MMTR_{t-5}]$$

It is clear that though the proportionate change in tax rate remains the same, the continuous time lag is involved i.e. t-1 [lagged by one year], t-2 [lagged by two years], t-3 [lagged by three years], t-4 [lagged by four years] and t-5] [lagged by five years] in estimating its impact on the income tax revenue whose proportionate change varies during post tax period.

The impact of reduction from 40 per cent [1996-97] to 30 per cent [1997-01] in MMTR on RIT is also concerned with the time lag [t – 1] as follows :

$$E_{1997\text{-}98} = [RIT_t - RIT_{t-1}/RIT_{t-1}] \;/\; MMTR_t - MMTR_{t-1}/MMTR_{t-1}]$$
$$E_{1998\text{-}99} = [RITt - RIT_{t-1}/RIT_{t-1}] \;/\; MMTR_t - MMTR_{t-2}/MMTR_{t-2}]$$
$$E_{1999\text{-}00} = [RITt - RIT_{t-1}/RIT_{t-1}] \;/\; MMTR_t - MMTR_{t-3}/MMTR_{t-3}]$$
$$E_{2000\text{-}01} = [RITt - RIT_{t-1}/RIT_{t-1}] \;/\; MMTR_t - MMTR_{t-4}/MMTR_{t-4}]$$

Here also the continuous time lag involved though the proportionate change in tax rate remains constant. As time lag increases, its quite common to expect a persistent increase in the magnitude of the elasticity of income tax revenue with respect to tax rates, all else equal.

12. The linear form of equation, $RIT = \beta_0 + \beta_1\, MMTR + error$, is also fitted to the data points to see the nature of buoyancy of income tax as follows :

    $dRIT/dGDP = \beta_1$ [which is the marginal income tax revenue of tax rate and constant.] > 0. The income tax buoyancy is calculated as follows :

    $$dRIT/dMMTR*\overline{GDP}/\ \overline{RIT} = \beta_{1*}\overline{GDP}/\ \overline{RIT}$$

13. This implies that the ratio of RIT to GDP declines as GDP increases.
14. This implies that the ratio of RIT to GDP increases as GDP increases.
15. The value of correlation coefficient lies between –1 and +1.
16. Published by Govt. of India, Ministry of finance, Economic Division.
17. Published by Govt. of India, Ministry of Finance, Department of Economic Affairs, Economic Division.
18. Special Statistics: Finances of Govt. of India, Economic and political Weekly Research Foundation, Vol. XXXVI, No. 14 and 15, April 14-20, 2001.

19. Published by Centre for Monitoring the Indian Economy, Bombay.

20. The results of the equation 1 fitted to the time series data are given below :

Income Tax Revenue Function - Results of Regression Analysis

Dependent Variable: RIT			
Method: Least Squares			
Sample: 1961 2001			
Included observations: 41			
Variable	*Coefficient*	*Std. Error*	*t-Statistic*
Constant	-1856.990	1332.555	-1.393556
GDP*	0.015592	0.000618	25.21373
T*	-126.3279	29.68460	-4.255670
MMTR	87.13809	60.04043	1.451324
$MMTR^2$	-0.599107	0.535208	-1.119392
R-squared	0.989239		
Adjusted R-squared	0.988044		
F-statistic	827.3906		
Durbin-Watson stat	1.087155		

Note: * Significant at 1% level.

21. Correlation Matrix

Variable	*RIT*	*GDP*	*TIME*	*MMTR*	*$MMTR^2$*
RIT	1.000000	0.990791	0.782541	-0.501120	-0.494056
GDP	0.990791	1.000000	0.831858	-0.516704	-0.517321
TIME	0.782541	0.831858	1.000000	-0.273487	-0.342214
MMTR	-0.501120	-0.516704	-0.273487	1.000000	0.984153
$MMTR^2$	-0.494056	-0.517321	-0.342214	0.984153	1.000000

22. dRIT/dMMTR [which is an absolute value of income tax revenue function] falls/rises as MMTR rises/falls. The optimal level of revenue from income tax at a particular tax rate can be worked out by setting dRIT/dMMTR = β_1-2β_2MMTR=0 [which is necessary condition to have optimal level of income tax revenue].

$\beta_1 = 2\beta_2$ MMTR

$\beta/2\beta_2 =$ MMTR

23 Which is sufficient condition to have optimal level of income tax revenue at particular tax rate.

***Post Script :** Since the data on income tax revenue and maximum marginal tax rates now are available till 2003, the quadratic equation [Equation 1a] to the data [for the forty three years - 1961-2003] is also fitted. The results of the same are given below:

Dependent Variable: Y				
Method: Least Squares				
Sample: 1961 2003				
Included observations: 43				
Variable	*Coefficient*	*Std. Error*	*t-Statistic*	*Prob.*
X1	541.6508	105.9797	5.110892	0.0000
$X1^2$	-7.281195	1.621847	-4.489446	0.0001
R-squared	0.173747			
Adjusted R-squared	0.153595			
Durbin-Watson statistic	0.109192			

So far as income tax revenue and its relationship with the maximum marginal tax rate was concerned, the sign of coefficient of marginal maximum tax rate turned out to be positively significant and that of its square negatively significant once again during 1961 - 2003 corroborating the earlier results emerged out of the data used for the period 1961 to 2001. As per the present estimates of coefficients of the maximum marginal tax rate and square of it, though the low value of goodness of fit is a matter of concern, an optimal maximum marginal income tax rate to maximize tax revenues from income tax is worked out to be 37 percent [541.6508/2 *7,281195 = 37] Since the present maximum marginal income tax rate is below this level, would an increase in maximum marginal tax rate from the present rate of 30 percent to 37 percent augment the revenues from income tax? This requires further empirical investigation by considering various aspects connected to income tax.

24. The size of the average elasticity of RIT with respect to MMTR [worked out from the estimated linear regression equation given below] is 2.14778

$$RIT = 52000.07 - 958.9317 \,[MMTR]$$
$$t = -3.7318$$
$$r^2 = 0.635$$

****Postscript:** The MMTR and RIT were moving in the opposite direction in all the years during post tax reform period [1992-2003] except for the year 1997-98 where they were in the same direction.

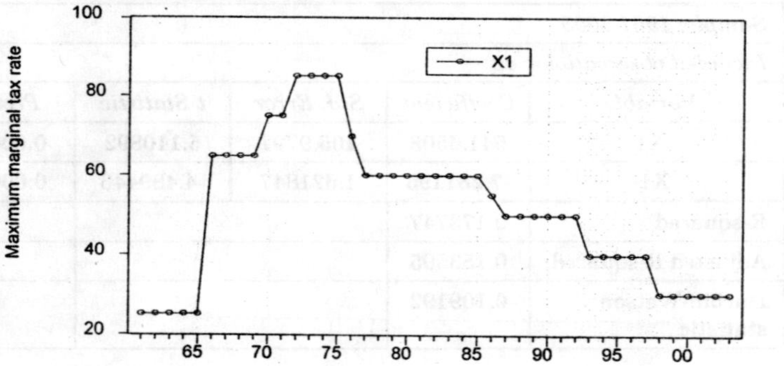

Fig. 7.8

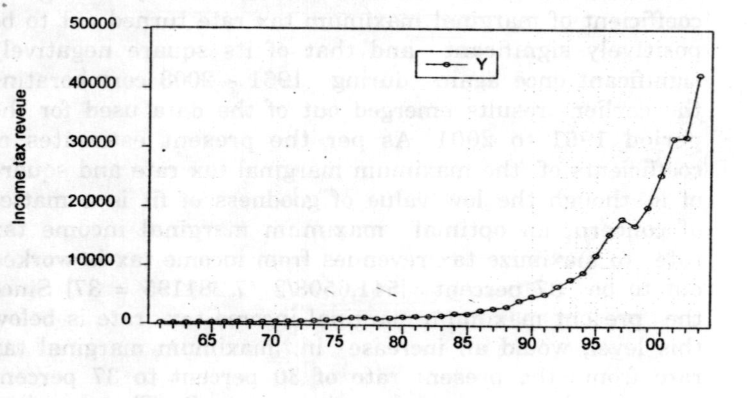

Fig. 7.9

25. Growth rate of RIT is estimated from the following equation

$$\ln RIT = 3.65098 - 0.16752\,T$$
$$t = 16.79$$
$$r^2 = 0.87263$$

26. Growth rate is estimated from the following equation

$$\ln MMTR = 5.872076 - 0.06348T$$
$$t = -7.403603$$
$$r^2 = 0.872639$$

27. The size of the average elasticity of RIT with respect to GDP [worked out from the estimated linear regression equation given below] is 1.21938

$$RIT = -3623.890 + 0.015208T$$
$$t = 14.5368$$
$$r^2 = 0.9783$$

28. The growth rate of GDP is estimated from the following equation

$$\ln GDP = 9.1782 + 0.1364T$$
$$t = 45.04$$
$$r^2 = 0.996$$

29. This can be seen from the following regression equations of 1) [RIT/GDP] on GDP

$$[RIT/GDP] = 0.009190 + 2.17E\text{-}09T$$
$$t = 3.412564$$
$$r^2 = 0.5927$$

and [RIT/GDP] on TIME

$$[RIT/GDP] = -0.001308 + 0.000377T$$
$$t = 3.429$$
$$r^2 = 0.5931$$

30. The following table shows the marginal maximum tax rate of income [payable by assesses in the top most slab] in developing and developed countries in 1999.

Developing countries	*Maximum Marginal Tax Rate [Per cent]*	*Developed countries*	*Maximum Marginal Tax Rate [Per cent]*
Hong Kong	17	Canada	29
Brazil	28	US and UK	40
India and Malaysia	30	Italy	46
Sri Lanka and Argentina	35	Australia	47
Thailand	37	Austria and Japan	50
South Korea	40	Germany	53
South Africa and China	45	Belgium	55
		Denmark	59
		Netherlands	60

Source: World Development Indicators, 2000, World Bank, Washington.

Among developing countries Hong Kong has a lowest rate of 17 per cent and South Africa and China have a high tax rate of 45 per cent. The rate of tax was moderate in India and Malaysia at 30 per cent each. Among developed countries the highest marginal tax rate was 60 per cent in Netherlands followed by Denmark with 59 per cent and Belgium with 55%. Canada has a lowest rate of 29 per cent.

References

Amaresh Bagchi, [1994]: "India's Tax Reforms: A Progress Report", *Economic and Political Weekly*, Vol. XXIX, No. 43, October 22. *American Economist*, Vol. 27(1).

Basu S.C., [1973]: "Revenue Buoyancy Allows W. Bengal a Tax Free Budget", *Yojana*, Vol. 17, No. 5.

Bender Bruce [1984]: "An Analysis of the Laffer Curve", *Economic Inquiry*, Vol. 22, July.

Bhat K. Sham, Kannabiran G., [1992]: "Measuring Elasticity and Buoyancy of Tax Revenue in Tamil Nadu : A Divisia Index Approach", *Prajnan*, Vol. 21, No. 2.

Buchanan, James M, Lee Dwight-R. [1982]: "Politics, Time, and the Laffer Curve", *Journal of Political Economy*, Vol. 90, August.

Claessens, Stijn, [1990]: "The debt Laffer Curve: Some Estimates", *World Development,* Vol. 18, December.

Clar, Jeff R. [1996]: "Sentencing Laffer Curves, Political Myopia, and Prison Space".

Clark, Jeff R. Lee, Dwight R. [1996]: "Sentencing Laffer Curves: Response to the Critics", *Social Science Quarterly*, Vol. 77, June.

Damodar Gujarati, [1999]: *Essentials of Econometrics*, Irwin McGraw – Hill, Singapore.

Dehejia, Vivek H. Rowe, Nicholas [1995]: "The Laffer Curve and Precautionary Taxation: A Rationale for Paying Down the National Debt", Australian Economic-Papers, Vol. 34, December.

Denicolo, Vincenzo [1988]: "Some Analytics of the Laffer Curve: A Comment", *Journal of Public Economics*, Vol. 35, February.

Dwivedi, D.N. [1976]: "A Buoyancy Approach to the Evaluation of Excise Taxation in India", *Indian-Economic Review*, Vol. 11, October.

Dwivedi, D.N., [1976]: "Elasticities and Buoyancy of Excise Taxation in India", *Indian Economic Review*, Vol. XI, No. 2 October, 1976.

Gahvari, Firouz [1988]: "Does the Laffer Curve Ever Slope Down", *National Tax Journal*, Vol. 41, June.

Gahvari, Firouz [1989]: "The Nature of Government Expenditures and the Shape of the Laffer", *Journal of Public Economics*, Vol. 40, November.

Govinda Rao, M [2000]: "Tax Reform in India: Achievements and Challenges", *Asia – Pacific Development Journal*, Vol. 7, No. 2, December.

Hsing, Yu [1996]: "Estimating the Laffer Curve and Policy Implications", *Journal of Socio-Economics*, Vol. 25.

Husain Aasim M. [1992]: "Distortionary Taxation and the Debt Laffer Curve", International Monetary Fund Working Paper, January.

Hussain, Aasim M. [1997]: "Domestic Taxes and the External Debt Laffer Curve", *Economica*, Vol. 64, August.

M.M. Sury, [1978]: "Elasticity of Tax Revenue: Some Measurement Problems", *The Indian Economic Journal*, Vol. 26.

Malcomson, James-M. [1986]: "Some Analytics of the Laffer Curve", *Journal of Public Economics*, Vol. 29, April.

Malcomson, James-M. [1988]:"Some Analytics of the Laffer Curve: a Comment", *Journal of Public Economics*, Vol. 35, February.

Mansfield, Charles Y. [1972]: "Elasticity and Buoyancy of a Tax System: A Method Applied to Paraguay", International-Monetary Fund Staff Papers, Vol. 19, July.

Purohit, M.C., [1978]: "Buoyancy and Income – Elasticity of State taxes in India", *Artha Vijnana*, Vol. 20, No. 5, September,

Rao, V.G. [1976] : *The Responsiveness of Tax System in India*, Allied, New Delhi.

Sahota, G.S. [1961]: Indian Tax Structure and Economic Development, Asia Publishing House, Bombay.

Sahota, G.S. [1991], Taxpayer Responsiveness to Changes in Income Tax Rates in India, Occasional Paper, No.10, August, National Institute of Public Finance and Policy, New Delhi.

Sen Kunal, [1992]: "A Laffer Curve in the Use of the Banking Sector for Budget Financing", *Journal for Quantitative Economics*, Vol. 8, No. 2.

Shapiro, Edward [1983], "Leisure-Income Indifference Curves and the Laffer Curve".

Singh Tejinder, Jain A.K., [2000]: "The Corporation Tax in India : Empirical Validity of Laffer Curve", *Finance India*, Vol. 14, No. 3.

Special Statistics: "Finances of Government of India [2001]", *Economic and Political Weekly*, Vol. XXXVI, Nos. 14 & 15, April 14-15.

Special Statistics: Finances of Government of India, [2002]: *Economic and Political Weekly*, Vol. XXXVII, Nos. 15, April 13-19.

Sury, M.M. [1985]: "Buoyancy and Elasticity of Union Excise Revenue in India 1950-51 to 1980-81", *Margin*, Vol. 18, October.

Swaminathan, [2001] : "Tax Agenda in the Melting Pot", *The Hindu* [Business], December 26.

Tax Buoyancy: Beyond Compliance, [1995]: *Economic and Political Weekly*, Vol. 30, No. 12.

Tax Reform Committee, Final Report, Part I August 1992.

Thomas J. Hailstones [1982]: *A Guide to Supply Side Economics*, Reston Publishing Company.

Upender, M. [1999]: "A Shift in the Buoyancy of the Indian Tax System : An Empirical Search", Prajnan, Vol. 28, No. 1.

Upender M., [1998]: "The Buoyancy of the Indian Tax Structure: An Exercise", *Prajnan*, Vol. 26, No. 4.

Upender, M. [2001]: "The Shift in the Magnitude of Economic Relationships", *Asian – African Journal of Economics and Econometrics*, Vol. 1, No. 1.

Waud, Roger N. [1988]: "Tax Aversion, Optional Tax Rates, and Indexation", *Public Finance*; Vol. 43.

Index